The Age of Innocence

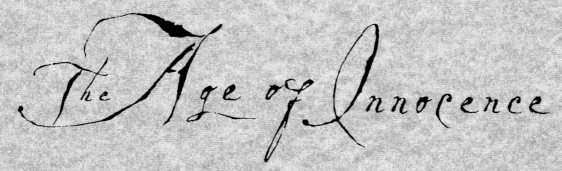

The Age of Innocence

A PORTRAIT OF THE FILM
BASED ON THE NOVEL BY EDITH WHARTON

MARTIN SCORSESE

JAY COCKS

EDITED BY ROBIN STANDEFER
PRODUCTION PHOTOGRAPHS BY PHILLIP V. CARUSO

NEWMARKET PRESS
NEW YORK

93 94 95 96   10 9 8 7 6 5 4 3 2 1

Library of Congress Cataloging-in-Publication Data

Scorsese, Martin.
The age of innocence : a portrait of the film / Martin Scorsese,
Jay Cocks ; edited by Robin Standefer.
p. cm.
Includes bibliographical references.
ISBN 1-55704-143-1 — ISBN 1-55704-142-3 (pbk.)
1. Age of innocence (Motion picture). 2. Wharton, Edith, 1862-1937. Age of innocence.
3. Wharton, Edith, 1862-1937—Film and video adaptations.
I. Cocks, Jay. II. Standefer, Robin. III. Title.
PN1997.A31183S26 1993
891.43'72—dc20

Quantity Purchases

Companies, professional groups, clubs, and other organizations may qualify for special terms when
ordering quantities of this title. For information, write Special Sales, Newmarket Press,
18 East 48th Street, New York, N.Y. 10017, or call (212) 832-3575.

Produced by Newmarket Productions, a division of
Newmarket Publishing & Communications Company:
Esther Margolis, director, Keith Hollaman, editor,
Joe Gannon, production manager, Eileen Max, production consultant.

BOOK DESIGN BY TANIA GARCIA

Interior hand-lettering by Craig DeCamps

Color separations by New Sele
Manufactured in Italy by L.E.G.O.

First Edition

page i: Unidentified women, *albumen print, cabinet card by Alman & Co., late 19th century*
page vi: The Wyndham Sisters: Lady Elcho, Mrs. Adeane, and Mrs. Tennant, *John Singer Sargent, 1899*

To our parents

— M.S.
— J.C.

Contents

have sometimes thought that a woman's nature is like a great house full of rooms: there is the hall, through which everyone passes in going in and out; the drawing room, where one receives formal visits; the sitting room, where the members of the family come and go as they list; but beyond that, far beyond, are other rooms, the handles of whose doors are never turned; no one knows the way to them, no one knows whither they lead; and in the innermost room, the holy of holies, the soul sits alone and waits for a footstep that never comes.

—*Edith Wharton, 1891*

Edith Wharton, ca. 1885

Introduction

To keep my balance, I had to remember what Marty said: "It's a love story. What's important is the feeling, not the setting. Just nail the emotion and everything else will follow." I didn't forget, but I did get dislocated, even on location. Especially there.

The first day of shooting *The Age of Innocence* was in mid-March, in a wintry field near an old stone house in rural New York. I had some small experience on locations, and had spent a little time around various video monitors, watching scenes on a black-and-white Sony as they played out in front of the movie camera. But I hadn't ever been so close to a movie before, been so much a part of it and had it be, for so long, a part of me, of so much that I dreamed and hoped. And there it was, suddenly in front of my eyes, happening.

I felt, in quick succession, everything I was supposed to: relief, excitement, elation. But then something new came into the mix, gradually at first, then quickly absorbing every other feeling inside itself. It seemed like confusion. And it felt like sadness.

I didn't know where it came from, and I managed, I think, to mask it. But, watching Daniel and Michelle on that monitor screen, hooded from the direct sunlight, I felt not only that we had found something right but that it was over. That we had discovered it, then left it behind before we had a chance to know fully what it was.

It was the monitor. What was a piece of vital utility to Marty and Michael Ballhaus became, to me, an unbidden vehicle into the near future. I wasn't seeing a film beginning on that screen. It was as if I was seeing something that had been finished without me, as if I'd woken from a dream and already forgotten the most glorious parts. The movie had been shot, edited, scored, released to theaters, and then on to video all in one great jump cut. And I'd missed it all.

Television was one of the most important ways Marty and I had gotten used to seeing movies, especially treasured movies, older movies we tried to learn from: They lived for us on the small, curved glass screen. There they were finished, inflexible, immutable. Movies on television were, for us, the equivalent of going to the library for research. And here, all too suddenly, I saw *The Age of Innocence*, done and, as it were, on the shelf of the past. In order to get my bearings on the movie still at hand, I had to deprogram myself of all the enforced melancholy of these fantasies, turn away from what I knew and whatever I'd expected.

It was then I understood the surprise—and, sometimes, skepticism—which I heard so often whenever, in the early days, the subject of our work on *The Age of Innocence* came up. It was all about dislocation. Marty and I had last worked together on *The Last Temptation of Christ,* as personal and emotional as any movie Marty has made, the closest, I believe, if not to his heart, then to his soul. That movie, with its passionate, obsessive, self-doubting Christ, may have been unorthodox, but it was at least consistent with the sort of risks Marty was used to taking and expected to take. It was also the sort of wild swing that I was believed, by those who knew us both, always to be urging my friend to take: Here, you go fight, I'll hold your coat.

But *Temptation* was one thing, *Innocence* another. When I was asked initially about the new movie, I expected that people might think we were playing it safe, doing a cakewalk. Instead, there seemed to be a undertow of interrogative doubt in every polite query and comment. I had one vivid preview of this before production began, when I met a literature professor who had gotten hold of our script. "I looked at the two names on the title page, and thought, 'What the hell is this?'" he told me. "One guy I never heard of, and another guy who makes gangster pictures. What do they know about this?" For him we were a Will Elder cartoon from a vintage *Mad*: a couple of low-born types who stomp into the Victorian parlor and blow their noses on the doilies.

Marty remained indifferent to anyone's preconceptions, and untroubled about what we knew going in. It was what we learned, coming out, along with what we felt throughout that he held most important. Movies, for Marty, are an investigation anyway; we could learn what we needed as we got deeper into the work. We had a single charter: "Nail the emotion." This was a love story requiring fineness and finesse, set among the first families and old order of New York. It was not something we were born to, but then, that might be an advantage. We could come to it without an agenda.

Both of us had responded to the quick of Wharton's novel—to the emotion—and not just to the decoration. We could both learn something from adapting such a book—something, for example, about precision of plotting—and, as we did that, lend something of our own. We wanted to bring the novel together with the spirit of the older movies we admired and, sometimes, loved (see the "Sources" section later in this book). If these disparate films shared something in common, it was a spirit of unwavering—indeed, in some cases, headlong—individuality. They were not paralyzed by the pedigree of their sources.

Classics tend to calcify into respectability. After years of academic approval and adaptation to multi-part public television series, an excess of good breeding settles over them like a thick layer of dust. Just as Newland Archer is stifled, then strangled by the strictures of his society, so do adaptations of uppercase literature tend to come giftwrapped in a dramatic gentility that mutes the hard edges of emotion. We wanted to try, anyway, to do something that was closer to the spirit of those honored older movies. We thought, learning from them, we might fashion a way of not only unwrapping the hard edges, but sharpening them so that they stabbed the heart, not just fluttered past it.

Marty knew that the story, evocative of a particular and fascinating time, was not after all peculiar to it. "The setting's important," he said, "only to show why this love is impossible." True, but the setting is seductive. I'd been seduced by it myself, immediately and irrevocably, when my college crony P. F. Kluge had passed the book along with a spare description of its splendors and a simple statement that it contained "one of the great last lines of dialogue." I had tapped the generosity and catholicity of Kluge's taste relentlessly, so I read the book right away. Each chapter flashed in front of me like reels of a film. But when I got around to giving Marty the book some years later, I let him find out about the dialogue himself. I went back to Sources. I held the book in my hand like a talisman and scattered some of those favorite movie titles in the air like motes of gold dust.

After many long years of movie-watching and movie-talking and occasional movie-making between us, Marty knew this was buff's shorthand, a way to suggest the ambiance and texture of a movie that might come to pass, not its possible stature. We would, if we were lucky, be casing an area we loved, not moving into the neighborhood. So I handed the book over and hoped hard for luck.

Then I waited a while. Marty put the novel on his shelf but put off reading it, as if by instinct, until an incident in his personal life sounded a resonance with Wharton's narrative. Then, all at once, he picked it up and saw it all.

Marty immediately saw those chapter-by-chapter reels, just as I did. And he saw more. He saw scenes. He saw shots. He saw camera moves. And he saw cuts. I think the whole movie was in his head by the time he turned the last page. While we eagerly began to share and explore all the book's possibilities, we also did a little research. We discovered *The Age of Innocence* had been dramatized on Broadway, with Katharine Cornell, in 1928, and subsequently filmed (this was news) as an early talkie with Irene Dunne and John Boles. The film, which we never managed to see, is obscure, but this would not have been a matter of moment to the author. Her interest in movies seems to have been as a marketplace, not as a medium. She sold rights to several of her works, including the short story "The Old Maid," which turned into the immemorial Bette Davis-Miriam Hopkins weepie, and *The Glimpses of the Moon*, a novel that became a silent success with the participation of the stars Bebe Daniels, Nita Naldi, and Maurice Costello, and with the collaboration of F. Scott Fitzgerald, who worked on the script.

Wharton's literary reputation had, over the years, lost some prominence, if not luster. Despite the exemplary efforts of her biographer, R. W. B. Lewis, and others, she was popularly imagined—if she was thought of at all—as a kind of Jamesian acolyte, a monied snob whose best-remembered work (*Ethan Frome*) was her least typical and shortest, known primarily because it showed up on secondary school reading lists. Coming to *Age* was like finding a treasure that had been lost through unfair neglect and misunderstanding. Its story was as vivid as its milieu was tangible. Reading it over repeatedly, scrawling marginal notes, we could feel its melancholy in our shared spirit even as we imagined the plot passing before our eyes, like a brougham emerging from the fog. We hailed the carriage, climbed in, and let it take us away.

Marty, with every new movie, was becoming ever more adept at rendering the shadings and exactitudes of various contemporary subcultures. His fierce eye for detail and his palpable evocation of social nuance would, I thought, have equally dazzling results turned to another time, a less familiar place. Here, I had an insider's edge. I knew my friend was an avid reader of history and was fascinated, as well, with social forms and rituals. This put the New York of Edith Wharton much closer to his hand than most people, who knew him through his work—or thought they did—might realize.

After twenty-two years of friendship, too, Marty and I had enough personal history together—some of it bruising—to have a sense of what lay close to each other's heart. Marty was well aware that I knew something of yearning and commitment, and something more about fear of risk, and loss, and personal havoc. For my own part, I was sure my friend had a clear eye for passion, a soul that, in all important things, was fearless, and a white-knuckle grasp of wayward love. Out of all this, shared and understood, a good movie might be started.

What seemed so obvious to two old friends was not quickly apparent to most anyone else. But we enjoyed taking everyone by surprise, and when the first draft of the script was finished in early February of 1989, after an intense and satisfying three weeks of work, the surprise was suddenly enhanced. To all those who read the script—everyone whose job it is to decide whether to make the film and whether to participate in it—surprise yielded to the attractive idea that this might be a different kind of Scorsese excursion, still personal yet rooted in an unfamiliar milieu, romantic but realistic. To our grateful relief, they began to share the possibility of our dream.

This book will give some sense, we hope, of how the dream worked out. It's our hope that, as you see the film and as you read the script here, you'll be taken up too by the precision of Wharton's narrative and the tangled, troubled essence of these characters whose story, set over a century ago, can still call us back so strongly into a tangible past. Yesteryear—that lovely antique word—should seem no longer ago than yesterday.

Of course, it was a giant step back to yesterday. There were prodigious amounts of research, planning, and designing to be done. And a good deal of additional writing, too. A second draft was finished in early December of 1991, and it was this version that Marty took into rehearsal with the principal actors. More changes were made when those several weeks of rehearsal ended. These usually involved dialogue adjustments, but, in one case, we imported two glistening cameo characters from the novel and gave them their heads for a few pages. These parts were cast but never shot. Because of time and length and the growing, awkward suspicion that their presence, amusing and intriguing as it may have been, was also diversionary, they were eliminated soon after shooting began. With regret.

The version of the script presented here, then, is the shooting script, with a little refurbishing. Some structural changes were made on the set, on the day—including a slippery modification of plot, involving a key and an envelope. These changes have been incorporated here, as have some of the dialogue deletions and emendations made during performance.

The ritual reminder/disclaimer has to be unfurled at this point: This script is not the finished movie. It is the thoroughfare by which the final movie was reached, and being a little longer and more meandering than demanded by strict specs, it is not necessarily the most direct route. We've made liberal use of narration. We both were beguiled by the formal beauty and wit of Wharton's language, its sculpted perfection, and wanted to include as much as possible. Marty was so intent on this that, on the set, he timed camera moves to the narration with hairsbreadth accuracy.

There were also lines of dialogue that seemed, on the page, to be an unfair challenge to the actors: words like "pantalettes," phrases like "draw it mild," that were fairly musty with period flavor but seemed to defy fleet contemporary exposition. Marty decided that they should remain as written, to see how they played. The actors, as it turned out, cherished the language; the confidence they drew from the rhythm and shading of the novel's dialogue seemed to anchor them. Much you will read, though, is still subject to change. As this is being written, film is being edited, the movie is finding its final form, and it is likely that there are things here that will not emerge on screen. We are still, now, in process.

The sections in the book which bracket and—we hope—complement the script should convey a notion, first, of how Edith Wharton's world was re-imagined and made real, and, then, act as an introduction to some of the people who fashioned it from the initial inspiration. We're not trying to lay out, start to finish, every step by which the movie was made. Rather, we're presenting a composite of the whole movie experience, passing along some idea of what struck and inspired all of us, what moved and directed and haunted us, and what helped us. These are images, ideas, fragments of thought that, somehow, made their way into the foundation of the film.

As Marty and I chose the pictures, worked with the layouts and found and fit the fragments of text, this book took on a more personal shading. It became a kind of family album, and, even more, the conclusion of the writing process: tracking back, rediscovering sources, redefining and refining the film on paper one last time before we let go. Even though I was invited to participate in the shooting of the film, and hovered eagerly, daily, over that video monitor, I'm still envious of the fine shaping and surgery that Marty, working with Thelma Schoonmaker, accomplishes with the huge raw celluloid manuscript brought forth after thirteen weeks of photography. Although he enjoys the challenging conviviality of shooting more than he likes to admit, Marty favors editing over all other aspects of filmmaking. "Editing, and writing," he said once. "That's what I like best." Both are actions of tempestuous exploration and refinement, focused and private. I think for Marty they are part of a single sweeping generative process in which the actual shooting becomes a kind of supercharged hiatus, to which I was a privileged participant.

On the best days—and they were numerous—we even lost our distance at the monitor. Marty, Michael Ballhaus, and I became, for the moment, enthusiastic spectators at a movie that seemed to have taken off by spontaneous generation. When the moment in front of us was particularly intense, it took Marty a little longer to call "Cut," and, when he did, you could hear, for a second, the scene's emotion in his voice. When the scene was more relaxed, we could respond accordingly. Watching Michelle arrange roses, the three of us laughed and clapped as the camera tracked around a platform which was circling in the opposite direction. Not missing a move while she spun on the platform, handling the stems with unflustered grace, her accent still in place and staying perfectly in character, Michelle said, "You guys need some popcorn."

It's not only the popcorn that is missing here. There are things I saw every evening in dailies, or in previews of the film-in-progress: the voices and bearing of our wonderful cast; all the tonality of light and camera movement; the rhythm of the edited film, the supportive strength of the music. Still. It is our hope you will find the core of the movie here, just as we searched for it as we wrote, during those first weeks, in Marty's apartment, high above Manhattan, looking out wide windows across the park and the concrete over a New York that was long past innocence.

"It's still out there," he said one day. "Maybe just the ghosts. But it's there." "Ghosts" had been mentioned in the novel, and so they found their way into the narration, by a kind of alchemical assimilation. All the writing would work like that: sudden swoops of inspiration followed by the fortifying dullness of routine. A computer, sternly silent, in one room, Marty and I in another, in as much isolation as can be enforced; talk about old movies; talk about the movie at hand, and not yet on paper; talk. There is no clear division of creative responsibility, except for the fact that I actually flog the keyboard and fret when the computer misbehaves; Marty gets to berate me for my high-tech preoccupations (as handy a work escape as any, and more practical than most) and make more phone calls. We both make the coffee.

Either of us can and might say anything. I can make Marty's visual ideas, detailed verbally in fine detail, work on the page, and also kick in the occasional camera idea; Marty is scrupulous about character behavior and nuance, and, in the case of *Age*, more protective even than I of Wharton's language. We both find ourselves, after a few days, discussing the characters as if they, not the computer, were waiting in the next room.

Marty can also be surprisingly, relentlessly specific, even in the early stages of work: It took us a good while, for example, to work out the servings for the Thanksgiving dinner scene and which character should be saying exactly what as the cranberry sauce is passed and spooned from which damn crystal dish. Then everything, sauce and all, is written down, read, discussed. Then there's more writing—occasionally a good deal more—and finally some initial result, subject to—expected to—change.

Sometimes I'll say, in answer to a casual question, that Marty and I are like musicians who have been playing together for over two decades; we can communicate, as musicians do, in a kind of terse shorthand, then follow and build on each other's solos. But I know, even while I'm saying it, that this is a rather romantic self-portrait, a corrective to that imaginary Will Elder cartoon. Secretly, I think that Marty and I, staring across the sky for inspiration, are really more like a couple of Sahara ostriches.

I doubt that Marty, whose animal obsessions run exclusively to a small white dog who makes a cameo appearance in *Age*, will cotton much to the comparison. But it's said that when thunderclouds appear, these desert ostriches will run, by instinct, toward the lightning. The flash reveals where the quick, intense rain, and the dousing sun that follows, will bring forth green grass to nourish and sustain until the next storm. And so it is, I think, with my friend and me: a couple of nomadic ostriches, hotfooting for the light across the shifting sand.

—J.C.

Preparation

They all lived in a kind of hieroglyphic world, where the real thing was never said or done or even thought, but only represented by a set of arbitrary signs.

—*Edith Wharton*, The Age of Innocence, *1920*

Fifth Avenue, 1875

21st Street at Fifth Avenue, 1870

There it is round you. Don't pass it by—the immediate, the real, the only, the yours, the novelist's that it waits for. Take hold of it and keep hold, and let it pull you where it will.... Do New York!

—Henry James, in a letter to Edith Wharton, 1902

Edith, Lady Playfair, *John Singer Sargent, 1884*   Madame Paul Poirson, *John Singer Sargent, 1885*

Arrangement in Flesh Color and Black: Portrait
of Théodore Duret, *James Abbott Whistler, 1883*

But the age was innocent in larger and more appreciable ways. If social engagements were all-absorbing, the pace was leisurely and the atmosphere decorous. One associated social life with the arrival of winter—the "season" began around the first of December—and one saw it, in retrospect, through a haze of snow. It seemed to snow more often in those New York winters, and the

14th Street, viewed from Fifth Avenue, during the blizzard of March 12, 1888

snow seemed to lie in cleaner heaps on the sidewalks than in later years. One of the regular diversions was to walk along Fifth Avenue or Broadway, well muffled, while snow swept down silently onto the roofs of the horsecars...

—*R. W. B. Lewis*, Edith Wharton: A Biography

Unidentified woman, *salt print, Mathew B. Brady, late 19th century*

It is impossible to separate people from their looks. A woman's natural quality is to attract, and having attracted, to enchain; and how influential she may be for good or for evil, the history of every age makes clear. We may add, therefore, that the culture of beauty is the natural right of every woman.

—*Mrs. H. R. Haweis,* The Art of Beauty, *1878*

Pink Faille Ball Toilette, *engraved illustration*
from Harper's Bazaar, *1876*

*T*he art of playing the Fan, in fact, can never be learnt; it
is innate in a woman of family, as are innate in her her least
gestures which captivate, her sweet childlike caresses, her speech,
her look, her walk.

—*Octave Uzanne,* The Fan, *late 19th century*

John William Casilear (1811-1898), *Asher B. Durand, ca. 1840*

$\mathcal{T}$he trouble with [young writers] is that they don't know
what a gentleman is, and after all it was a useful standard to
get one's perspective by.

—*Edith Wharton, to a friend*

*N*ew York was a metropolis, and perfectly aware that in metropolises it was "not the thing" to arrive early at the Opera; and what was or was not "the thing" played a part as

important in Newland Archer's New York as the inscrutable totem terrors that had ruled the destinies of his forefathers thousands of years ago.

—*Edith Wharton*, The Age of Innocence, *1920*

The Meeting of Faust and Marguerite in the Garden, *James Tissot, 1861*

*A*n unalterable and unquestioned law of the musical world required that the German text of the French operas sung by Swedish artists should be translated into Italian for the clearer understanding of English-speaking audiences. This seemed as natural to Newland Archer as all the other conventions on which his life was moulded.

—*Edith Wharton,* The Age of Innocence, *1920*

The Beaufort house was one that New Yorkers were proud to show to foreigners, especially on the night of the annual ball. The Beauforts had been among the first people in New York

to own their own red velvet carpet and have it rolled down the steps by their own footmen, under their own awning, instead of hiring it with the supper and the ball-room chairs.

—Edith Wharton, The Age of Innocence, *1920*

Too Early, *James Tissot, 1873*

It is not necessary to recognise a ball-room aquaintance the next day, unless you choose to do so. The introduction is for a dance, and not for future aquaintanceship. To act on it

afterwards depends entirely on the will of the lady; and she is not
ill-bred if she ignores her partner's existence the next day.

—Daily Duties of a House Mother, *1872*

*D*ress is the second self, a dumb self, yet a most eloquent expositor of the person. Dress bears the same relation to the body as speech does to the brain; and therefore dress may be called the speech of the body.

—*Mrs. H. R. Haweis,*
The Art of Beauty, *1878*

Evening Dress, Jacques Doucet, ca. 1902

Left: La Mondaine, *James Tissot, 1883*
Right: The Reception, *James Tissot, 1883*

Jeune femme à l'éventail, *James Tissot, 1870*

True womanhood includes all the delicate refinements that overflow in the perfect glove, the well-fitting shoe, the pretty stocking, the neat frills, the becoming bonnet. The American woman, to do her only justice, is a neat creature by instinct, and if she occasionally gives too much thought to dress, she is still to be admired and commended for her daintiness.

—The American Code of Manners, *1880*

et dress and a proper care for it ought not to minister merely to vanity, nor impair in any degree the moral tone. A woman ought to care what she wears for her own sake and for the sake of those about her. It is a fault, not a virtue, to be reckless as to the impression one leaves on the eye, just as it is a fault to be indifferent to the feelings of others.

—*Mrs. H. R. Haweis,* The Art of Beauty, *1878*

Modern Amazons, *woodblock taken from the drawing of Lucien Davis, late 19th century*

*I*n shooting at the target the first thing is to nock the arrow, that is, to place it properly on the string. In order to effect this, take the bow in the left hand, with the string toward you, the upper limb being toward the right.

The feet must be flat on the ground, with the heels a little apart, the left foot turned toward the mark. The head and chest inclined a little forward so as to present a full bust, but not bent at or below the waist.

The lady archers are apt to feel a little lame after the first two or three essays, but they should practise a short time every morning, and always in a loose waist or jacket.

—*M. E. W. Sherwood,* The Art of Entertaining, *1839*

A new era then came in: old fashions passed away, new ones replaced them. The French *chef* then literally, for the first time, made his appearance, and artistic dinners replaced the old-fashioned, solid repasts of the earlier period. We imported European habits and customs rapidly.

—*Ward McAllister,* Society as I Have Found It, *1890*

DINNER BILL OF FARE (*WINTER*).

Oysters served in block of ice.
Julienne soup (can purchase it canned).
Soft-shell crabs.
Sweet-breads; tomato-sauce.
Braised pigeons, with spinach.
Fillet of beef; sauce Hollandaise.
Roman punch, in lemon-skins.
Fillets of ducks, larded; poivrade-sauce; salad of vegetables.
French canned string-beans *(haricots verts)*
sautéd with butter, served on toast.
Macaroni, with cheese.
Maraschino Bavarian cream.
Chocolate-pudding, iced.
Fruits.
Coffee.

—*Mrs. Mary F. Henderson.*
Practical Cooking, and Dinner Giving, *1877*

Dinner at Haddo House, *Alfred C. Emslie, 1884*

$\mathcal{B}$y cultivating practices of refined dining, social conservatives presented an alternative model of social incorporation and growth....Diners might properly enjoy abundance, but the appetites were satisfied in a quiet and orderly way, and the cool control of intellect never faltered for an instant. The ritual structure of Victorian table manners mediated between contending needs that were central to the maintenance of social order: between individual appetite and communal order, bodily satisfaction and social modesty, egalitarianism and hierarchy, public and private.

—Dining in America: 1850-1890

$\mathscr{B}$ut to know about good cooking was a part of every young wife's equipment, and my mother's favourite cookery books (Francatelli's and Mrs. Leslie's) are thickly interleaved with sheets of yellowing note paper.

—*Edith Wharton,* A Backward Glance, *1934*

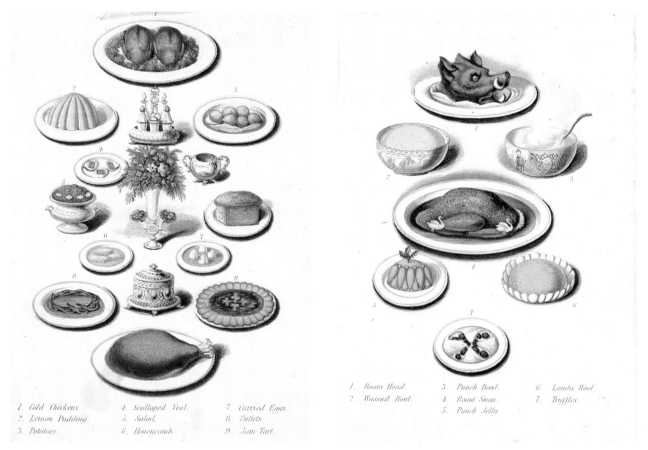

1. *Cold Chickens*. 4. *Scalloped Veal*. 7. *Curried Eggs*.
2. *Lemon Pudding*. 5. *Salad*. 8. *Cutlets*.
3. *Potatoes*. 6. *Honeycomb*. 9. *Jam Tart*.

1. *Boars Head*. 3. *Punch Bowl*. 6. *Lambs Wool*.
2. *Wassail Bowl*. 4. *Roast Swan*. 7. *Truffles*.
5. *Punch Jelly*.

Late 19th century book plates

To Roast Canvas-Back Duck

Having trussed the ducks, put into each a piece of soft bread that has been soaked in port wine. Place them before a quick fire and roast them from three quarters to an hour. Before they go to table, squeeze over each the juice of a lemon or orange, and serve them up very hot with their own gravy about them. Eat them with currant jelly. Have ready also, a gravy made by stewing slowly in a sauce-pan the giblets of the ducks in butter rolled in flour, and as little water as possible. Serve up this additional gravy in a boat.

—*Eliza Leslie*, Miss Leslie's New Cookery Book, *1857*

Newland Archer prided himself on his knowledge of Italian art. But these pictures bewildered him, for they were like nothing that he was accustomed to look at (and therefore able to see) when he travelled in Italy; and perhaps, also, his powers of observation were impaired by the oddness of finding himself in this strange empty house...

—*Edith Wharton*, The Age of Innocence, *1920*

Sarah Bernhardt's Winter Garden 1879, *Louise Abbema, 1879*

$\mathcal{W}$herein, then, lay the resemblance that made the young man's heart beat with a kind of retrospective excitement? It seemed to be in Madame Olenska's mysterious faculty of suggesting tragic and moving possibilities outside the daily run of experience. She had hardly ever said a word to him to produce this impression, but it was a part of her, either a projection of her mysterious and outlandish background or of something inherently dramatic, passionate and unusual in herself.

—*Edith Wharton,* The Age of Innocence, *1920*

La Liseuse, *Georges Croegaert, 1848*

Georges Croegaert · Paris · 1888

Unidentified bride, *albumen print, late 19th century*

The idea of revealing the bride to the mob of dressmakers and newspaper reporters who stood outside fighting to get near, exceeded even old Catherine's courage, though for a moment she had weighed the possibility. "Why, they might take a photograph of my child *and put it in the papers!*" Mrs. Welland exclaimed when her mother's last plan was hinted to her; and from this unthinkable indecency the clan recoiled with a collective shudder.

—*Edith Wharton,* The Age of Innocence, *1920*

Unidentified man, *albumen print,*
cabinet card by Roseti, late 19th century

Unidentified gentleman,
cabinet card by Sarony, late 19th century

Falk

949 BROADWAY, N.Y.

Emma Thursby, *albumen print,
cabinet card by Falk, late 19th century*

Gallery of the Louvre, *Samuel Morse, 1831*

*O*ur surroundings being then important, both for the cultivation of the eye and for the enhancement of our own inner and outer self, we naturally turn to the great army of artists to tell us what to do.

Alas, our artists hang back. They only paint pictures, and carve statues, of scenes and forms of visionary beauty, which they have not taught us to assimilate in any way—which they do not expect us to assimilate—only to pay for.

—*Mrs. H. R. Haweis,* The Art of Beauty, *1878*

Parisian Interieur, *Mihály Munkácsy, late 19th century*

The burden of Mrs. Manson Mingott's flesh had long since made it impossible for her to go up and down stairs, and with characteristic independence she had made her reception rooms upstairs and established herself (in flagrant violation of all the New York proprieties) on the ground floor of her house; so that, as you sat in her sitting room window with her, you caught (through a door that was always open, and a looped-back yellow damask portière) the unexpected vista of a bedroom with a huge

Bedroom in the residence of Mrs. A. T. Stewart, *illustration from* Artistic Houses, *1882*

low bed upholstered like a sofa, and a toilet-table with frivolous lace flounces and a gilt-framed mirror.

Her visitors were startled and fascinated by the foreignness of this arrangement, which recalled scenes in French fiction, and architectural incentives to immortality such as the simple American had never dreamed of.

—*Edith Wharton,* The Age of Innocence, *1920*

That roses and pinks, violets and lilacs, are suitable, goes without saying, for they are always delightful; but the heavy tropical odors of jasmine, orange-blossom, hyacinth, and tuberose should be avoided. A very pretty decoration is obtained by using flowers of one color, such as Jacqueminot roses, or scarlet carnations, which, if placed in the gleaming crystal glass, produce a very brilliant and beautiful effect.

—*Mrs. John Sherwood*, Manners and Social Usages, *1887*

Flowers, Chalice, Raspberries, *Jean Baptiste Robie, ca. 1880*

23rd Street at intersection of Broadway and Fifth Avenue, 1880

Between 1875 and 1900 New York changed from a comfortable town where all one's friends lived within walking distance and where one met them all day walking or driving, into a great city extending for miles and housing thousands of people of all nationalities.

—*Nathalie Dana*, Young in New York:
A Memoir of Victorian Girlhood

A gentleman will always be polite, in the parlor, dining-room, and in the street.

In a crowd, never rudely push aside those who impede your progress, but wait patiently until the way is clear. If you are hurried by business of importance or an engagement, you will find that a few courteous words will open the way before you more quickly than the most violent pushing and loud talking.

—*Cecil B. Hartley*, The Gentlemen's Book of
Etiquette and Fashion, *1872*

Library of the Residence of Edward N. Dickerson, *photograph from* Artistic Houses, *late 19th century*

H. J. Montague and Ada Dyas in a scene from The Shaughraun, *ca. 1874*

MOLINEUX: Forget what I've done! I'll go away; I'll never see you again.

CLAIRE: Don't go. I forgive you on one condition.

MOLINEUX: I accept it, whatever it may be.

CLAIRE: Never speak a word of love to me again.

—The Shaughraun, *Dion Boucicault, 1874*

I dreamt I dwelt in marble halls
with vassels and serfs at my side,
and of all who assembled within those walls
that I was the hope and the pride.

I dreamt that suitors sought my hand,
that knights upon bended knee
and with vows no maiden's heart could withstand,
they pledged their faith to me.
And I dreamt that one of that noble host
come forth my hand to claim.
But I also dreamt which charmed me most
that you loved me still the same

—*Michael William Both*, Marble Halls, *1852*

The Metropolitan Museum of Art, late 19th century

*Y*ou never did ask each other anything, did you? And you never told each other anything. You just sat and watched each other, and guessed at what was going on underneath.

—*Edith Wharton,* The Age of Innocence, *1920*

There is no such thing as growing old. There is only sadness.

—Edith Wharton, in a letter to a friend

The Adaptation

INT. THEATRE NIGHT

New York in the late 1870s.

A bunch of daisies makes a sudden sunburst of
BRIGHT YELLOW. A hand comes into frame, begins
to sprinkle petals on the ground. CAMERA tilts down
to follow petals and we see part of a woman's shoe.
It is strangely ornate, like something from an
Arabian Nights fantasy.

INT. THEATRE NIGHT
New York in the late 1870s.
A bunch of daisies makes a sudden sunburst of BRIGHT YELLOW. A hand comes into frame, begins to sprinkle petals on the ground. CAMERA tilts down to follow petals and we see part of a woman's shoe. It is strangely ornate, like something from an Arabian Nights fantasy.

As this is happening, we hear a burst of a dramatic music, and a voice singing an aria.

CAMERA pans up from the petals to the extravagantly painted face of a woman singer performing an aria from *Faust*.

PANNING continues through a series of DISSOLVES gradually revealing that we are on stage in a theater, the Academy of Music, in the latter part of the 19th century. The stage setting—of which we see only small portions—is elaborately painted. The footlights are CANDLES. Just past them, we see the orchestra, and past the orchestra, a glimpse of a full theater, lit by LIMELIGHT.

Continue PANNING AND DISSOLVING through a series of EXTREME CLOSE UPS of DETAILS of period evening wear: high collars, flowing ties, beautiful beading on dresses, jewelry on necks and wrists, men's cufflinks against immaculate white cotton shirts, and shoes...women's heels, men's black patent leather pumps.

PANNING AND DISSOLVING continues through the theater audience, past the slightly shabby red and gold painted boxes, ending briefly on the plain red velvet wall of a box.

Newland Archer enters. What we see of him first is the perfect gardenia attached to the lapel of his jacket. CAMERA pans up to his face. He is in his late 20s. Handsome, assured and guarded. He steps toward the front of the box, joining the company of several men, including Larry Lefferts who is approximately Newland's age, and Sillerton Jackson, who is older by a couple of decades.

Newland's move toward the front of the box is covered in TIGHT SHOTS. We still do not have a full view of the theater, and will not for the rest of this scene.

Lefferts looks at stage through pearl opera glasses. We see his POV: tight, of the stage, and the singer performing. FLASH PAN off singer through the audience, moving so fast it gives an almost kaleidoscopic impression of rich fabric and glittering jewels. Now we're back to Lefferts, who SWINGS opera glasses away from stage and toward another box.

He SEES: the figure of a woman entering a box across the way. Although the woman, silhouetted against candles, is still indistinct and mysterious to us, he recognizes her and reacts with controlled surprise.

LEFFERTS
Well.

He hands the glasses to Sillerton Jackson, who looks in the same direction. Newland watches Jackson, who takes the glasses away from his eyes after a moment and hands them back to Lefferts.

JACKSON
I didn't think the Mingotts would have tried it on.

The men in the box all stare, then turn away and look back at the stage: all but Newland. His glance FIXES on the figure of the woman in the box, who we still do not see clearly. The conversation of the men in his own box annoys him, but his face betrays a hint of something more than irritation. The sight of the woman in the box distracts him. Affects him.

LEFFERTS
Parading her at the opera like that. Sitting her next to May Welland. It's all very odd.

JACKSON
Well, she's had such an odd life.

LEFFERTS
Will they even bring her to the Beauforts' ball, do you suppose?

JACKSON
If they do, the talk will be of little else.

Archer looks at his companions in the box with just a suggestion of impatience. Then he turns and leaves.

                                        Cut to

INT. THEATER NIGHT
A corridor, decorated with old prints hung from a

red velvet wall and bright with candlelight.

Archer's POV as he moves quickly down the corridor, past doors leading to the boxes.

Archer stops at one of the doors and enters purposefully.

Cut to

INT. THEATER NIGHT

The box which had so interested the men. We see first what Archer notices: a BOUQUET of lilies-of-the-valley.

TILT UP to the lovely young face of May Welland as she turns, smiling, to greet Archer. She is radiant. Archer smiles back at her, and at her mother, seated beside her.

ARCHER
May. Mrs. Welland. Good evening.

MRS. WELLAND
Newland. You know my niece Countess Olenska.

We see the back of the Countess' head, her curly brown hair held in place around her temples by a narrow band of diamonds. She TURNS into close-up: this is clearly the figure who drew the attention of Lefferts and Jackson. She wears a distinctive blue velvet gown. Her face is unconventional, but it is magic.

Archer bows with the suggestion of reserve. Countess Olenska replies with a nod.

Newland sits beside May and speaks softly.

ARCHER
I hope you've told Madame Olenska.

MAY
(teasing)
What?

ARCHER
That we're engaged. I want everybody to know. Let me announce it this evening at the ball.

85

MAY

If you can persuade Mamma. But why should we change what is already settled?

He has no answer for this...no answer, anyway, that is appropriate for this time and place. May senses his frustration, and adds, smiling...

MAY

But you can tell my cousin yourself. She remembers you.

Countess Olenska turns.

ELLEN (COUNTESS OLENSKA)

I remember we played together. Being here again makes me remember so much.

She gestures out, and we PAN with her across the regal gathering: this is the first wide view we have had of the theater.

ELLEN

I see everybody the same way, dressed in knickerbockers and pantalettes.

Archer moves to sit beside her.

ELLEN

You were horrid. You kissed me once behind a door. But it was your cousin Vandy, the one who never looked at me, I was in love with.

Archer is a little taken aback.

ARCHER

Yes, you have been away a very long time.

Camera starts to move in as she raises a large fan of eagle feathers.

ELLEN

Oh, centuries and centuries. So long I'm sure I'm dead and buried, and this dear old place is heaven.

Fast cut to

MAIN TITLES
As they end, the voice of a WOMAN NARRATOR fades up and we...

Cut to

INT. THEATER NIGHT
In another box, the handsome Mrs. Julius Beaufort

(Regina) draws her opera cloak about her sculpted shoulders. As she does this, and leaves the box, we hear...

NARRATOR (V.O.)

It invariably happened, as everything happened in those days, in the same way. As usual, Mrs. Julius Beaufort appeared just before the Jewel Song and, again as usual, rose at the end of the third act and disappeared. New York then knew that, a half-hour later, her annual opera ball would begin.

Cut to

EXT. STREET OUTSIDE THEATER (14TH STREET) NIGHT
A line of carriages drawn up in front of the Academy of Music. Mrs. Beaufort climbs in a carriage at the front of the line and drives away.

NARRATOR (V.O.)

Carriages waited at the curb for the entire performance. It was widely known in New York, but never acknowledged, that Americans want to get away from amusement even more quickly than they want to get to it.

Cut to

INT. BALLROOM/BEAUFORT HOUSE NIGHT
Dark and empty, as it is on every other night of the year. CAMERA pulls back from CHANDELIER covered in a bag.

NARRATOR (V.O.)

The Beauforts' house was one of the few in New York that possessed a ballroom. Such a room, shuttered in darkness three hundred and sixty-four days of the year, was felt to compensate for whatever was regrettable in the Beaufort past. Regina Beaufort came from an old South Carolina family, but her husband Julius, who passed for an Englishman, was known to have dissipated habits, a bitter tongue and mysterious antecedents. His marriage assured him a social position, but not necessarily respect.

Through a series of DISSOLVES, the room suddenly comes to life. Gilt chairs are set out. The chandelier BLAZES with CANDLELIGHT. An orchestra plays. Dancers swoop by.

CAMERA tracks quickly along the carpet as people walk by, stopping at the front door. TILT UP from feet of an arriving guest: Newland Archer hands his opera cape to a servant and walks straight into large CLOSE-UP, which blacks out the camera.

Cut to

INT. HALL, STAIRS AND DRAWING ROOMS/BEAUFORT HOUSE

Archer hands his cape and hat to a servant, greets another guest and accepts several pair of dancing gloves, which rest on a table, each set identified with its own handwritten name card. CAMERA stays with Archer as he climbs the stairs....

...greets Regina Beaufort, who stands at the top of the stairs beneath an ornately-framed portrait of herself...

...and through the first drawing room, which is sea-green.

NARRATOR (V.O.)

The house had been boldly planned. Instead of squeezing through a narrow passage to get to the ballroom one marched solemnly down a vista of enfiladed drawing rooms....

Camera TRACKS with Archer, snaking around to show him now in profile, now again from the back, revealing details of the room and other guests moving through the opulent interior.

NARRATOR (V.O.)

...seeing from afar the many-candled lusters reflected in the polished parquetry and beyond that the depths of a conservatory...

Camera still TRACKS with Archer, moving all around him, as he enters the second drawing room, which is crimson.

NARRATOR (V.O.)

...where camellias and tree ferns arched their costly foliage over seats of black and gold bamboo. But only by actually passing through the crimson drawing room could one see "Return of Spring," the much-discussed nude by Bouguereau, which Beaufort had had the audacity to hang in plain sight.

CAMERA PANS OFF Archer, onto the voluptuous Bouguereau canvas, then back to Archer as he slows his step to take it in while still proceeding to the door of...the third drawing room. He crosses the threshold and starts across the room toward the ballroom.

NARRATOR (V.O.)

Archer had not gone back to his club after the Opera, as young men usually did, but had walked for some distance up Fifth Avenue before turning back in the direction of the Beauforts'. He was definitely afraid that the family might be going too far and would bring the Countess Olenska. He was more than ever determined to "see the thing through," but he felt less chivalrously inclined to defend the Countess after their brief talk at the opera.

As Archer enters the light and movement of the ballroom, we...

Cut to

INT. BALLROOM/BEAUFORT HOUSE

Start on Archer's POV as he enters the party and merges with the guests. The first man he sees is Larry Lefferts, deep in conversation with an attractive young woman.

ANGLE on Lefferts. Action slows (double-framing).

NARRATOR (V.O.)

On the whole, Lawrence Lefferts was the foremost authority on "form" in New York. On the question of pumps versus patent-leather Oxfords, his authority had never been disputed.

Double-framing ends. Resume normal action as Archer's POV continues through the party. Holding court and amusing a small group of older women is Sillerton Jackson.

ANGLE on Jackson. Action slows again (double-framing).

NARRATOR (V.O.)

Old Mr. Sillerton Jackson was as great an authority on "family" as Lawrence Lefferts was on "form." In addition to a forest of family trees, he carried a register of the scandals and mysteries that had smouldered under the unruffled surface of society for the last fifty years.

Double-framing ends. Resume normal action with Archer's POV moving through the party. Julius Beaufort, good-looking with a hint of flashiness, crosses in front of him, conversing with a guest.

GUEST
(in mid-discussion)
But I didn't see you there this evening. Madame Nilsson was in such splendid voice.

BEAUFORT
(snide)
The usual splendor, I'm sure.

ANGLE on Beaufort. Action SLOWS (double-framing)

NARRATOR (V.O.)
Julius Beaufort had speedily made a name for himself in the world of affairs. His secret, all were agreed, was the way he carried things off. His social obligations and the rumors that perpetually swirled around him, all were borne easily before him.

Double-framing ENDS. Resume normal action. CAMERA swings to another part of the room, concentrating now on May Welland surrounded by gleeful friends who are obviously reacting to her engagement announcement.
CAMERA moves into close-up of May. She looks up, smiles, extends her hand.
Now we see her POV of Archer kissing her hand.

Cut to

INT. CONSERVATORY/BEAUFORT HOUSE NIGHT
Another room. Behind a tall screen of tree ferns and camellias, Archer presses May's gloved HAND to his lips.

MAY
You see, I told all my friends. Just as you asked.

ARCHER
Yes, I couldn't wait. Only I wish it hadn't had to be at a ball.

MAY
Yes, I know. But after all, even here we're alone together, aren't we?

ARCHER
Always. The worst of it is...

He takes a quick look around the room: no one's nearby.

ARCHER
...that I want to kiss you and I can't.

But he does. He steals a furtive kiss, which pleases and surprises May. They walk to a sofa, which affords a bit of privacy, and sit. In CLOSE-UP, Archer absently breaks off a piece of lily-of-the-valley from her bouquet.

MAY
Did you tell Ellen, as I asked you?

ARCHER
No. I didn't have the chance after all.

MAY
She's my cousin, if others know before she does...It's just that she's been away for so long that she's rather sensitive.

ARCHER
Of course I'll tell her, dearest. But I haven't seen her yet.

MAY
She decided not to come at the last minute.

ARCHER
At the last minute?

MAY
She was afraid her dress wasn't smart enough. We all thought it was so lovely, but she asked my aunt to take her home.

ARCHER
Oh well.

He smiles.

Cut to

INT. BALLROOM/BEAUFORT HOUSE NIGHT
May smiling back. But now she is moving giddily around the ballroom floor, swept up in the rhythm

of a WALTZ. The background behind her is a blur.

REVERSE shot of Archer, swirling along with her, returning her smile.

Now they both join the flow of the other dancers, all partners in a great social pageant.

HIGH OVERHEAD ANGLE, looking down: on the entire ballroom below, dancers all turning together in a rhythmic tableaux.

Cut to

INT. SITTING ROOM DAY

Waltz music echoes out. We start on a CLOSE-UP of an engagement ring: a large thick sapphire set in invisible claws. We hear the hearty, admiring voice of Mrs. Manson Mingott as we start to DISSOLVE.

MRS. MINGOTT

Very handsome. Very liberal. In my time a cameo set in pearls was thought to be sufficient.

DISSOLVE ends on medium-shot of Mrs. Mingott. She is hugely fat, as vast and august as a natural phenomenon, but her eyes are vibrant, and miss nothing.

May Welland, Mrs. Welland and Archer sit close by Mrs. Mingott, whose girth is supported by a careful arrangement of silk pillows very near a window from which she can confidently watch society come to call.

MRS. WELLAND

It's the new setting. Of course it shows the stone beautifully, but it looks a little bare to old-fashioned eyes.

MRS. MINGOTT

I hope you don't mean mine, my dear. I like all the novelties. But it's the hand that sets off the ring, isn't it, my dear Mr. Archer? My hands were modeled in Paris by the great Rocheé. He should do May's.

She reaches out for May's hand.

MRS. MINGOTT

Her hand is tempered. It's these modern sports that spread the joints. But the skin is white.
(staring straight at Archer)

And when's the wedding to be?

MRS. WELLAND
(a little flustered)
Oh...

ARCHER
(jumping in)
As soon as ever it can. If only you'll back me up, Mrs. Mingott.

MRS. WELLAND
(recovering)
We must give them time to know each other a little better, mamma.

MRS. MINGOTT
Know each other? Everybody in New York has always known everybody. Don't wait till the bubble's off the wine. Marry them before Lent. I may catch pneumonia any winter now, and I want to give the wedding breakfast.

As everyone reacts to Mrs. Mingott's statement with surprise and (at least in Archer's case) pleasure, SOUND fades down as they continue to talk and we hear the voice of the...

NARRATOR (V.O.)
Mrs. Manson Mingott was, of course, the first to receive the required betrothal visit. Much of New York was already related to her, and she knew the remainder by marriage or by reputation. Though brownstone was the norm, she lived magisterially within a large house of controversial pale cream-colored stone, in an inaccessible wilderness near the Central Park.

As narration continues, CAMERA moves freely around the Mingott house, showing us rooms and giving an impression of secure wealth and unquestioned power.

NARRATOR (V.O.)
The burden of her flesh had long since made it impossible for her to go up and down stairs. So with characteristic independence she had established herself on the ground floor of her house. From her sitting room, there was an unexpected vista of her bedroom.

CAMERA EXPLORES the unusual geometry of Mrs. Mingott's living quarters as narration continues.

NARRATOR (V.O.)
Her visitors were startled and fascinated by the foreignness of this arrangement, which recalled scenes in French fiction. This was how women with lovers lived in the wicked old societies. But if Mrs. Mingott had wanted a lover, the intrepid woman would have had him too.

CAMERA now moves up a long set of stairs, past a gallery of ornately-framed PICTURES. We DISSOLVE from painting to painting, and from EXTREME CLOSE-UPS of details in each, as narration continues.

NARRATOR (V.O.)
But she was content, at this moment in her life, simply to sit in a window of her sitting room, waiting calmly for life and fashion to flow northward to her solitary doors, for her patience was equalled by her confidence.

DISSOLVE FROM image in painting to Archer, May and Mrs. Welland, standing up to say their goodbyes. (Narration concludes over farewells.)
As they finish speaking, a door opens behind them and CAMERA MOVES IN on
Ellen Olenska and Julius Beaufort entering, just as the other guests are leaving.

MRS. MINGOTT
Beaufort! This is a rare favor.

She holds out her hand to Beaufort as the others greet each other. Beaufort moves toward Mrs. Mingott.

BEAUFORT
Unnecessarily rare, I'd say. But I met Countess Ellen in Madison Square, and she was good enough to let me walk home with her.

MRS. MINGOTT
This house will be merrier now that she's here.

Push up that tuffet. I want a good gossip.

Archer and the Welland women drift out into the hall under Ellen's guidance, as Beaufort remains behind, conversing with Mrs. Mingott.

May and her Mother put on their furs.

Ellen looks at Archer with a faintly questioning smile.

ARCHER

(laughing shyly)
Of course you already know. About May and me. She scolded me for not telling you at the opera.

ELLEN

Of course I know. And I'm so glad. One doesn't tell such news first in a crowd.

May and Mrs. Welland are at the door. Ellen holds her hand out to Archer.

ELLEN

Good-bye. Come and see me some day.

Archer looks at her.

Cut to

EXT. MINGOTT HOUSE DAY

As Archer follows May and her mother into their waiting carriage.

MRS. WELLAND

It's a mistake for Ellen to be seen parading up Fifth Avenue with Julius Beaufort at the crowded hour. The very day after her arrival...

The carriage pulls away from the curb.

Cut to

INT. DINING ROOM/ARCHER HOUSE NIGHT

Newland Archer is having dinner with his mother Adeline, sister Janey, and Sillerton Jackson.

Start CLOSE on a piece of meat being probed gently with a knife and fork as if it were a lab specimen. TILT UP to see Sillerton Jackson looking at his filet with skepticism and resignation as we hear...

NARRATOR (V.O.)

Mrs. Archer and her daughter Janey were both shy women and shrank from society. But they liked to be well informed of its doings.

CAMERA pans to Janey and Mrs. Archer as Jackson speaks.

JACKSON

(in midst of holding forth)
Certain nuances escape Beaufort.

MRS. ARCHER

Oh, necessarily. Beaufort is a vulgar man.

ARCHER

Nevertheless, no business nuances escape him. Most of New York trusts him with its affairs.

MRS. ARCHER

My grandfather Newland always used to say to mother, "Don't let that fellow Beaufort be introduced to the girls." But at least he's had the advantage of associating with gentlemen. Even in England, they say. It's all very mysterious.

As dinner conversation continues, SOUND fades down and we hear...

NARRATOR (V.O.)

As far back as anyone could remember, New York had been divided into two great clans. Among the Mingotts you could dine on canvasback duck, terrapin and vintage wines. At the Archers, you could talk about Alpine scenery and "The Marble Faun" but receive tepid Veuve Cliquot without a year and warmed-up croquettes from Philadelphia.

JANEY

And the Countess Olenska...was she at the ball too?

MRS. ARCHER

I appreciate the Mingotts wanting to support her, and have her at the opera. I admire their esprit de corps. But why my son's engagement should be mixed up with that woman's comings and goings I don't see.

JACKSON

Well, in any case, she was not at the ball.

93

MRS. ARCHER

At least she had that decency.

A butler offers mushroom sauce to Jackson, who sniffs almost imperceptibly and motions the butler away. Jackson glances at the portraits of the Archer family antecedents on the wall, and fixes on one of a well-fed, slightly flush older man. He looks over at Archer, who is watching him with bemused understanding.

JACKSON

(can't resist)
Ah, how your grandfather appreciated a good meal, Newland.

JANEY

I wonder if she wears a round hat or a bonnet in the afternoon. The dress she wore to the opera was so plain and flat...

MRS. ARCHER

Yes, I'm sure it was in better taste not to go to the ball.

ARCHER

I don't think it was a question of taste, mother. May said the countess decided her dress wasn't smart enough.

MRS. ARCHER

Poor Ellen. We must always remember what an eccentric bringing-up Medora Manson gave her. What can you expect of a girl who was allowed to wear black satin at her coming-out ball?

JANEY

It's odd she should have kept such an ugly name as Ellen when she married the Count. I should have changed it to Elaine.

ARCHER

Why?

JANEY

I don't know. It sounds more...Polish.

MRS. ARCHER

It certainly sounds more conspicuous. And that can hardly be what she wishes.

ARCHER

(argumentative)
Why not? Why shouldn't she be conspicuous if she chooses? She made an awful marriage, but should she hide her head as if it were her fault? Should she go slinking around as if she'd disgraced herself? She's had an unhappy life, but that doesn't make her an outcast.

JACKSON

I'm sure that's the line the Mingotts mean to take.

ARCHER

I don't have to wait for their cue, if that's what you mean, sir.

MRS. ARCHER

(trying to cool things out)
I'm told she's looking for a house. She means to live here.

JANEY

I hear she means to get a divorce.

ARCHER

I hope she will.

Cut to

INT. STUDY/ARCHER HOUSE NIGHT
CLOSE on a cigar being passed.
Jackson accepts the cigar from Archer and both men light up after dinner.

JACKSON

There are the rumors, too.

ARCHER

I've heard them. About the secretary?

JACKSON

He helped her get away from the husband. They say the Count kept her practically a prisoner.
(shrugs)
Certainly, the Count had his own way of life.

ARCHER

You knew him?

JACKSON

I heard of him at Nice. Handsome, they say, but eyes with a lot of lashes. When he wasn't with women he was collecting china. Paying any price for both, I understand.

ARCHER

Then where's the blame? Any one of us, under the same circumstances, would have helped the Countess, just as the secretary did.

JACKSON

He was still helping her a year later, then, because somebody met them living together at Lausanne.

ARCHER

(reddening slightly)
Living together? Well why not? Who has the right to make her life over if she hasn't? Why should we bury a woman alive if her husband prefers to live with whores?

JACKSON

Oh, it's hardly a question of entombment. The Countess is here, after all. Or do you believe that women should share the same freedoms as men?

ARCHER

(with some force)
I suppose I do. Yes, I do.

Jackson draws on his cigar.

JACKSON

Well, apparently Count Olenski also takes a similarly modern view. I've never heard of him lifting a finger to get his wife back.

Cut to

MONTAGE
Of heavy vellum envelopes, written in beautiful calligraphy, being passed from hand to hand and delivered on silver plates; of invitations being drawn from the envelopes.

NARRATOR (V.O.)

Three days later, the unthinkable happened.
Mrs. Manson Mingott sent out invitations
summoning everyone to a "formal dinner."
Such an occasion demanded the most careful
consideration. It required the appropriate
plate...

We see Mrs. Mingott with members of her
housekeeping staff, selecting china and silver from
FOLIOS: large leather binders filled with sketches of
plates, glasses, bowls, dishes, serving utensils and silver.

NARRATOR (V.O.)

It also called for three extra footmen, two
dishes for each course and a Roman punch
in the middle.

As these items are mentioned, we see them in the
montage: the footmen; the fancy food; the brimming
bowl of punch; kitchen staff busily preparing a feast.

NARRATOR (V.O.)

The dinner, New York read on the invitation, was "to meet the Countess Olenska."
And New York declined.

Montage ends on image of the kitchen staff DIS-
SOLVING away, leaving the kitchen empty.

Cut to

INT. DRAWING ROOM/ARCHER HOUSE DAY

Mrs. Archer angrily detailing the slight to the
family as Janey and Archer attend her.

MRS. ARCHER

"Regret." "Unable to accept." Without a
single explanation or excuse. Even some of
our own. No one even cares enough to conceal their feeling about the Countess. This is
a disgrace. For our whole family. And an awful blow to Catherine Mingott.

Archer is seen now in CLOSE-UP as he watches his
mother. Her voice fades down and we hear...

NARRATOR (V.O.)

They all lived in a kind of hieroglyphic
world.

As the narrator speaks, Archer imagines Ellen,
seeing her quickly...

...looking through the cards of refusal. The words
loom large: "Cannot." "Regret." "Must decline." But
each of these rebuffs is sent on a different, luxurious
piece of stationary, each written in a beautiful but
strikingly different hand. She sorts through the invitations, which FLIP past fast, like pages in an old flip
book. Ellen's face loses its usual composure. Now she
turns her head...

NARRATOR (V.O.)

The real thing was never said or done or
even thought, but only represented by a set
of arbitrary signs. These signs were not always subtle, and all the more significant for
that. The refusals were more than a simple
snubbing. They were an eradication.

... and Archer's image of Ellen fades on that last
dreadful word: "eradication."

We are back in the drawing room. Mrs. Archer
has reached a decision and has risen from her seat.

MRS. ARCHER

Don't tell me all this modern newspaper
rubbish about a New York aristocracy. This
city has always been a commercial commu-
nity, and there are not more than three families in it who can claim an aristocratic ori-
gin in the real sense of the word. Even dear
Mr. Welland made his money in enterprise.
So. (looking at them with resolution)
We will take up this matter with the van der
Luydens.

She starts for the door.

MRS. ARCHER

You should come with me, Newland. Louisa
van der Luyden is fond of you, and of course
it's on account of May we're doing this.

ARCHER

Of course.

MRS. ARCHER

If we don't all stand together, there'll be no such
thing as society left.

Cut to

INT. DRAWING ROOM/VAN DER LUYDEN HOUSE

DAY

Start on a tight-shot of the patrician Henry van der Luyden and his wife Louisa. They have the same pale blue eyes, with the same look of frozen gentleness. They look calmly at Archer and his mother before them.

HENRY

And all this, you think, was due to some intentional interference by...

ARCHER

...Larry Lefferts, yes sir. I'm certain of it.

LOUISA

But why?

We are in a high-ceilinged white-walled room in the Madison Avenue house of the van der Luydens.

A framed Gainsborough and a Huntington portrait of Louisa van der Luyden hang prominently.

ARCHER

Well. Excuse me, but...

LOUISA

Please, go on.

ARCHER

Larry's been going it harder than usual lately. Some service person in their village or someone, and it's getting noticed. Whenever poor Gertrude Lefferts begins to suspect something about her husband, Larry starts making some great diversionary fuss to show how moral he is. He's simply using Countess Olenska as a lightning rod.

LOUISA

Extraordinary.

HENRY

    Not at all, my dear, I'm afraid.

MRS. ARCHER

    We all felt this slight on the Countess should not pass without consulting you.

HENRY

    Well, it's the principle that I dislike. I mean to say, as long as a member of a well-known family is backed by that family, it should be considered final.

LOUISA

    It seems so to me.

HENRY

    So with Louisa's permission...and with Catherine Mingott's, of course...we are giving a little dinner for our cousin the Duke of St. Austrey, who arrives next week on the *Russia*. I'm sure Louisa will be as glad as I am if Countess Olenska will let us include her among our guests.

Cut to

HALLWAY AND DRAWING ROOM/VAN DER LUY-DEN HOUSE

    Start on Ellen's ungloved hand as she fastens a BRACELET around her wrist while she walks up the curving marble stairs toward the closed doors of the drawing room.

NARRATOR (V.O.)

    The occasion was a solemn one and the Countess Olenska arrived rather late. Yet she entered without any appearance of haste or embarrassment the drawing room in which New York's most chosen company was somewhat awfully assembled.

    Servants open the drawing room doors and Ellen enters unhurriedly, still securing her bracelet. Without embarrassment or self-consciousness, she looks back at the judgmental faces of New York's elite arrayed before her. Save for Archer, the guests are all older than Ellen by a couple of decades, and the weight of their judgement hangs heavy in the air.

    Henry and Louisa van der Luyden come forward

simultaneously and bring Ellen around the room, making introductions. As the Countess meets each redoubtable guest, we...

Cut to

INT. DINING ROOM/VAN DER LUYDEN HOUSE NIGHT

    A formidable dinner party is in progress. Start with CLOSE UP of wine being poured into glistening crystal decanters on a sideboard. CAMERA MOVES PAST the decanters to see what else is on the sideboard: heavy, elegant silver forks, knives, spoons, and other even larger, more formidable pieces used for serving; delicate glassware; wine coolers of hand-engraved silver.

NARRATOR (V.O.)

    The van der Luydens stood above all the city's families. They dwelled in a kind of super-terrestrial twilight, and dining with them was at best no light matter. Dining there with a Duke who was their cousin was almost a religious solemnity.

    DISSOLVE to elegant dinnerware on the sideboard, CAMERA STILL MOVING. As these items are mentioned in the narration, we see details of PATTERNS on each, as they DISSOLVE from one to another while the CAMERA GLIDES past.

NARRATOR (V.O.)

    The Trevenna George II plate was out. So was the van der Luyden Lowestoft, from the East India Company, and the Dagonet Crown Derby.

    CUT to a plate of Maine oysters being consumed by a dinner guest from a delicate majolica plate.

    CUT to footman, carving fish at the side table.

    CUT to a plate of fine du Lac Sèvres being placed on the table in front of another guest.

NARRATOR (V.O.)

    When the van der Luydens chose, they knew how to give a lesson.

    CUT to the centerpiece of the dinner table. We DOLLY IN ON an epergne laden with flowers and CASCADING WATER.

    On the dolly in, MUSIC SWELLS and SOUNDS of

dinner conversation become more prominent.

Cut to EXTREME CLOSE-UP of an individual ice mold on a guest's plate. (This signifies a change in the dinner course.)

Cut to a direct OVERHEAD SHOT of the whole long table in the grand room.

Cut to a FOUR SHOT of Mrs. van der Luyden, Archer, his mother, and the Duke, a rather taciturn fellow with expansive whiskers, all conversing at the table. The Duke is seated to his hostess' immediate right.

WHIP PAN down the table to Ellen Olenska. She is radiant.

Archer looks down the table at her as we...

Cut to

INT. DRAWING ROOM/ VAN DER LUYDEN HOUSE NIGHT

Crowded with guests, all enjoying themselves.

Archer, seated on a sofa, continues to look at Ellen Olenska, who is in easy conversation with the Duke across the room. She seems to have thawed out the visitor a good deal. As Archer watches, she gets up and starts across the room.

Archer keeps WATCHING: will she come toward him?

NARRATOR (V.O.)

It was not the custom in New York drawing rooms for a lady to get up and walk away from one gentleman in order to seek the company of another.

As Archer watches her progress across the room, she does seem to be coming right toward him.

NARRATOR (V.O.)

But the Countess did not observe this rule.

She is next to Archer now, smiling as she sits beside him.

ELLEN

I want you to talk to me about May.

ARCHER

You knew the Duke before?

ELLEN

From Nice. We used to see him every win-

ter. He's very fond of gambling and used to come to our house a great deal. I think he's the dullest man I ever met.

Archer smiles, delighted at her outspokenness.

ELLEN

But he's admired here. I suppose he must seem the very image of traditional Europe. Can I tell you, though...
(mock conspiratorial)
...what most interests me about New York? It's that nothing has to be traditional here. All this blind obeying of tradition...somebody else's tradition...is thoroughly needless. It seems stupid to have discovered America only to make it a copy of another country. Do you suppose Christopher Columbus would have taken all that trouble just to go to the opera with Larry Lefferts?

ARCHER

(laughs)
I think if he knew Lefferts was here the *Santa Maria* would never have left port.

ELLEN

And May. Does she share these views?

ARCHER

If she does, she'd never say so.

ELLEN

Are you very much in love with her?

ARCHER

As much as a man can be.

ELLEN

Do you think there's a limit?

ARCHER

If there is, I haven't found it.

ELLEN

Ah, it's really and truly a romance, then. Not in the least arranged.

ARCHER

Have you forgotten? In our country we don't allow marriages to be arranged.

ELLEN

Yes, I forgot, I'm sorry, I sometimes make these mistakes. I don't always remember that everything here is good that was...that was bad where I came from.

Her lips tremble. She looks down in her lap, at her FAN of eagle feathers.

ARCHER

I'm so sorry. But you are among friends here, you know.

ELLEN

Yes, I know. That's why I came home.

She glances toward the door, where May, dressed in a gown of silver and white, is entering with her mother. Several men, including the Duke, come up to them. Introductions are made.

ELLEN

You'll want to be with May.

ARCHER

(looking at the men around May)
She's already surrounded. I have so many rivals.

ELLEN

Then stay with me a little longer.

And she TOUCHES his knee lightly with her PLUMED FAN.

ARCHER

Yes.

But they are interrupted by Henry van der Luyden and a GUEST.

HENRY

Countess, if I may. Mr. Urban Dagonet.

Ellen smiles and Archer gets up to yield his place. Ellen holds her hand out to him.

ELLEN

Tomorrow then. After five. I'll expect you.
Archer manages to conceal his surprise.

ARCHER

Tomorrow.

And the Countess turns her attention to van der Luyden and the guest. As Archer walks away from her, he sees Larry Lefferts bringing his wife Gertrude over for an introduction.

Now Louisa van der Luyden falls into step beside Archer.

LOUISA

It was good of you to devote yourself to Madame Olenska so unselfishly, dear Newland. I told Henry he really must rescue you.

She looks around with satisfaction at the glittering gathering.

LOUISA

I think I've never seen May looking lovelier. The Duke thinks her the handsomest woman in the room.

He catches May's eye. She is indeed beautiful. They smile at each other.

Cut to

INT. DRAWING ROOM/ELLEN'S HOUSE DAY

Start on a large painting, more daring and more modern than any art we have seen up to now.

Archer stares at it, a little uncertain, a little puzzled.

Another painting, by a different artist but much like the first in its subject matter and the unsettling intensity of its mood.

Archer looks away from this second painting to some of the odd bits of furnishing in the room: small slender tables of dark wood, a stretch of red damask nailed on the discolored wallpaper, a delicate little Greek bronze.

He hears a noise in the hall. A Sicilian maid walks by the door. Archer looks at her. The maid speaks no English but understands his unspoken question.

MAID

Verra, verra.

"Soon, soon." Archer understands, but this does little to lessen his impatience.

He hears the sound of a horse moving down the street. He gets up, moves to the window and parts the curtains.

Looking out, he sees: a compact English

BROUGHAM, drawn by a big roan, stopping at the curb. The carriage door opens and Julius Beaufort climbs down. He turns, and helps the Countess out.

As Archer watches, Beaufort, hat in hand, says something to Ellen. She shakes her head. They shake hands and part. Beaufort climbs back into the carriage. Ellen comes up her front steps.

Archer turns away from the window. Ellen comes into the room, taking off her hat and long cloak as she moves toward him.

ELLEN

Do you like this odd little house? To me it's like heaven.

ARCHER

(reaching for the right compliment)
You've arranged it delightfully.

ELLEN

Yes. Some of the things I managed to bring with me. Little pieces of wreckage. At least it's less gloomy than the van der Luydens', and not so difficult to be alone.

ARCHER

(smiles)
I'm sure it's often thought the van der Luydens' is gloomy, though I've never heard it said before. But do you really like to be alone?

ELLEN

As long as my friends keep me from being lonely.

She sits near the fire and motions him to sit in an armchair near where he is standing.

103

ELLEN

I see you've already chosen your corner.

As he sits, she folds her arms behind her head and stares at the fire.

ELLEN

This is the hour I like best, don't you?

ARCHER

I was afraid you'd forgotten the hour. I'm sure Beaufort can be very intriguing.

ELLEN

He took me to see some houses. I'm told I must move, even though this street seems perfectly respectable.

ARCHER

Yes, but it's not fashionable.

ELLEN

Is fashion such a serious consideration?

ARCHER

Among people who have nothing more serious to consider.

ELLEN

And how would these people consider my street?

ARCHER

(lightly, disparagingly)
Oh, well, fleetingly, I'm afraid. Look at your neighbors. Dressmakers. Bird stuffers. Cafe owners.

ELLEN

(smiling)
I'll count on you to always let me know about such important things.

The maid enters with a tray of tea, which she sets in front of Ellen.

ARCHER

The van der Luydens do nothing by halves. All New York laid itself out for you last night.

ELLEN

It was so kind. Such a nice party.

She busies herself with serving the tea. Archer wants to impress on her the importance of the van der Luydens' gesture.

ARCHER

The van der Luydens are the most powerful influence in New York society. And they receive very seldom, because of cousin Louisa's health.

ELLEN

Perhaps that's the reason then.

ARCHER

The reason?

ELLEN

For their influence. They make themselves so rare.

Her observation intrigues him. She watches him as she hands him tea. The FIRELIGHT makes her eyes gleam.

ELLEN

But of course you must tell me.

ARCHER

No, it's you telling me.

She detaches a small gold cigarette case from one of her bracelets, holds it out to him. He takes a cigarette and she removes one for herself before closing the case.

ELLEN

Then we can both help each other. Just tell me what to do.

A flame darts from the logs in the fireplace. She bends over the fire. As Archer watches, she stretches her hand so close to the flame that it seems a faint halo of light shines around her fingernails. The firelight turns the dark hair escaping from her braids to russet and makes her pale skin even paler.

ARCHER

There are so many people already to tell you what to do.

ELLEN

They're all a little angry with me, I think.

104

For setting up for myself.

ARCHER

Still, your family can advise you...show you the way.

ELLEN

Is New York such a labyrinth? I thought it was so straight up and down, like Fifth Avenue, with all the cross-streets numbered and big honest labels on everything.

ARCHER

Everything is labeled. But everybody is not.

ELLEN

There are only two people here who make me think they can help and understand. You and Mr. Beaufort.

ARCHER

(reacts to mention of Beaufort)
I understand. Just don't let go of your old friends' hands so quickly.

ELLEN

Then I must count on you for warnings, too.

ARCHER

All the older women like and admire you. They want to help.

ELLEN

Oh, I know, I know. But only if they don't hear anything unpleasant. Does no one here want to know the truth, Mr. Archer? The real loneliness is living among all these kind people who only ask you to pretend.

She puts her hands to her face and SOBS. Her shoulders shake. Archer goes to her quickly, bending over her.

ARCHER

No, no, you musn't. Madame Olenska.

He takes her hands.

ARCHER

Ellen.

This is the first time he's called her by her first name, and it makes him a little self-conscious. He holds her HAND and rubs it back and forth, like a child's.

After a moment she draws her hand away and starts to compose herself.

ELLEN

No one cries here, either? I suppose there's no need to.

Cut to

EXT./INT. STREET AND FLORIST EVENING
Walking home from Ellen's along Fifth Avenue, Archer passes a flower shop. He gets only a few steps beyond it, then turns and goes back.

Inside the shop, the florist greets him instantly.

FLORIST

Oh Mr. Archer, good evening. We didn't see you this morning, and weren't sure whether to send Miss Welland the usual...

ARCHER

The lilies-of-the-valley, yes. We'd better make it a standing order.

He notices a cluster of YELLOW ROSES almost fiery in their beauty.

ARCHER

And those roses. I'll give you another address.

He draws out a CARD and places it inside an envelope, on which he starts to write Ellen's name and address. But he stops. He removes his card and hands the clerk the EMPTY ENVELOPE with only the name and address on it.

ARCHER

They'll go at once?

In extreme CLOSE-UP, Archer folds his calling card in two and places it safely in his pocket.

Cut to

MONTAGE
A series of rapidly DISSOLVING images: of the maid's hands on the yellow roses as they are delivered; of Ellen's more delicate hands arranging the roses in a vase; of Ellen's face, looking at roses, turning toward CAMERA.

Cut to

INT. AVIARY DAY

The WINGS of a bird fly past the CAMERA as Archer and May walk among the cages.

MAY

It's wonderful to wake every morning with lilies-of-the-valley in my room. It's like being with you.

ARCHER

They came late yesterday, I know. Somehow the time got away from me.

MAY

Still, you always remember.

ARCHER

I sent some roses to your cousin Ellen, too. Was that right?

MAY

Very right. She didn't mention it at lunch today, though. She said she'd gotten wonderful orchids from Mr. Beaufort and a whole hamper of carnations from Cousin Henry van der Luyden. She was so very delighted. Don't people send flowers in Europe?

He seems mildly annoyed at this. Suddenly the glorious tail of a PEACOCK spreads across the frame as we...

Cut to

INT. AVIARY DAY

As Archer and May sit on bench among the imposing cages.

MAY

Well, I know you do consider it a long time.

ARCHER

Very long.

MAY

But the Chivers were engaged for a year and a half. Larry Lefferts and Gertrude were engaged for two. I'm sure Mama expects something customary.

ARCHER

Ever since you were little your parents let

you have your way. You're almost twenty-two. Just tell your mother what you want.

MAY

But that's why it would be so difficult. I couldn't refuse her the very last thing she'd ever ask of me as a little girl.

ARCHER

Can't you and I just strike out for ourselves, May?

MAY

(laughing lightly)
Shall we elope?

ARCHER

If you would.

She TOUCHES his arm.

MAY

You do love me, Newland. I'm so happy.

ARCHER

Why not be happier?

MAY

I couldn't be happier, dearest. Did I tell you I showed Ellen the ring you chose? She thinks it's the most beautiful setting she ever saw. She said there was nothing like it in the rue de la Paix.

She hugs his arm.

MAY

I do love you, Newland. Everything you do is so special.

Cut to

INT. DINING ROOM/HOUSE NIGHT

The congenial, slightly florid face of Mr. Letterblair looks straight into CAMERA.

LETTERBLAIR

Countess Olenska wants to sue her husband for divorce. It's been suggested that she means to marry again, although she denies it.

Angle on Archer, most uncomfortable.

ARCHER

I beg your pardon, sir. But because of my en-

gagement, perhaps one of the other members of our firm could consider the matter.

LETTERBLAIR

But precisely because of your prospective alliance...and considering that several members of the family have already asked for you...I'd like you to consider the case.

ARCHER

It's a family matter. Perhaps it's best settled by the family.

LETTERBLAIR

Oh their position is clear. They are entirely, and rightly, against a divorce. But Countess Olenska still insists on a legal opinion.

Cut to

INT. DINING ROOM/LETTERBLAIR HOUSE NIGHT
CAMERA follows a bowl of oyster soup as it is being served.

LETTERBLAIR (V.O.)

But really, what's the use of a divorce? She's here, he's there and the whole Atlantic's between them.

FAST DISSOLVE to next course being served: shad and cucumbers.

LETTERBLAIR (V.O.)

As things go, Olenski's acted generously. He's already returned some of her money without being asked.

Another FAST DISSOLVE, to next course: young broiled turkey with corn fritters.

LETTERBLAIR (V.O.)

She'll never get a dollar more than that. Although I understand she attaches no importance to the money, other than the support it provides for Medora Manson.

Another FAST DISSOLVE to the final course: canvas-

108

back duck with currant jelly and a celery mayonnaise.

LETTERBLAIR (V.O.)

Considering all that, the wisest thing really is to do as the family says. Just let well enough alone.

Fast PAN up to Archer.

ARCHER

I think that's for her to decide.

Cut to

INT. LIBRARY/LETTERBLAIR HOUSE

START on EXTREME CLOSE-UP of an exceptionally fine pair of small GOLD SCISSORS neatly clipping the end of a cigar.

CUT TO CLOSE-UP of the edge of the cigar being lit.

CUT TO CLOSE-UP of Letterblair puffing on the cigar.

LETTERBLAIR

Have you considered the consequences if the Countess decides for divorce?

CUT TO TWO-SHOT of Letterblair and Archer seated comfortably in the library, where a fire is lit.

ARCHER

Consequences for the Countess?

LETTERBLAIR

For everyone.

ARCHER

I don't think the Count's accusations amount to anything more than vague charges.

LETTERBLAIR

It will make for some talk.

ARCHER

Well I have heard talk about the Countess and her secretary. I heard it even before I read the legal papers.

LETTERBLAIR

It's certain to be unpleasant.

ARCHER

Unpleasant!

Letterblair looks at him enquiringly and gives him a moment to calm down.

LETTERBLAIR

Divorce is always unpleasant. Don't you agree?

ARCHER

Naturally.

LETTERBLAIR

Then I can count on you. The family can count on you. You'll use your influence against the divorce?

ARCHER

I can't promise that. Not until I see the Countess.

LETTERBLAIR

I don't understand you, Mr. Archer.

Archer reaches into his pocket and pulls out one of his cards, along with a gold pencil. He starts to write a brief MESSAGE on the back.

LETTERBLAIR

Do you want to marry into a family with a scandalous divorce suit hanging over it?

ARCHER

I don't think that has anything to do with the case.

He finishes the note.

ARCHER

Can someone take this for me, please. To the Countess.

CAMERA in close on note, of which we see, in extreme CLOSE-UP, a few crucial words: "important"; "see"; "soonest."

Cut to

INT. FOYER/ELLEN'S HOUSE NIGHT

The maid opens the front door to admit Archer. He enters and takes off his hat and coat, walking into tight CLOSE-UP. He spots something in the foyer.

We see, as he does: on a bench, in the hallway, a sable-lined overcoat and a folded opera hat. We move closer in a very fast series of DISSOLVES until we see:

the dull silk lining of the hat, and the initials J. B. sewn in gold.

Archer reacts to this, and to voices behind him. He turns, and sees Ellen coming from the drawing room accompanied by Julius Beaufort.

BEAUFORT

Three days at Skuytercliff with the van der Luydens! You'd better take your fur and a hot water bottle.

ELLEN

Is the house that cold?

She holds her hand out to Archer in greeting as she speaks.

BEAUFORT

No, but Louisa is.

He nods carelessly at Archer.

BEAUFORT

Join me at Delmonicos Sunday instead. I'm having a nice oyster supper, in your honor.

The maid helps him on with his coat.

BEAUFORT

Private room, congenial company. Artists and so on.

ELLEN

That's very tempting. I haven't met a single artist since I've been here.

ARCHER

I know one or two painters I could bring to see you, if you'd allow me.

BEAUFORT

Painters? Are there any painters in New York?

ELLEN

(smiling)
Thank you. But I was really thinking of singers, actors, musicians. Dramatic artists. There were always so many in my husband's house.
(to Beaufort)
Can I write tomorrow and let you know? It's

too late to decide this evening.

BEAUFORT

Is this late?

ELLEN

Yes, because I still have to talk business with Mr. Archer.

BEAUFORT

Oh.
He starts to leave, but turns.

BEAUFORT

Of course, Newland, if you can persuade the Countess to change her mind about Sunday, you can join us too.

He leaves and the maid closes the door firmly behind him.

Cut to

INT. DRAWING ROOM/ELLEN'S HOUSE NIGHT
Archer sits closes, across from her, in an armchair.

ELLEN

You know painters, then? You live in their milieu?

ARCHER

Oh, not exactly.

ELLEN

But you care for such things?

ARCHER

Immensely. When I'm in Paris or London I never miss an exhibition. I try to keep up.

ELLEN

I used to care immensely too. My life was full of such things. But now I want to cast off all my old life...to become a complete American and try to be like everybody else.

ARCHER

You'll never be like everybody else.

ELLEN

Don't say that to me, please. I just want to put all the old things behind me.

ARCHER

I know. Mr. Letterblair told me.

ELLEN

Mr. Letterblair?

ARCHER

Yes. I've come because he asked me to. I'm in the firm.

ELLEN

You mean it's you who'll manage everything for me? I can talk to you? That's so much easier.

ARCHER

Yes... I'm here to talk about it. I've read all the legal papers, and the letter from the Count.

ELLEN

It was vile.

He notices her hands, sees she's wearing THREE RINGS on her third and fourth fingers. But there is no wedding ring. He says, as he's noticing...

ARCHER (V.O.)

But if he chooses to fight the case, he can say things that might be unpleas...

His glance comes back up to her face.

ARCHER

...might be disagreeable to you. Say them publicly, so that they could be damaging even if...

ELLEN

If?

ARCHER

Even if they were unfounded.

ELLEN

What harm could accusations like that do me here?

ARCHER

Perhaps more harm than anywhere else. Our legislation favors divorce. But our social customs don't.

A small travel clock TICKS on the table beside her.

ELLEN

Yes. So my family tells me. Our family. You'll be my cousin soon. And you agree with them?

ARCHER

If what your husband hints is true, or you have no way of disproving it...yes. What could you possibly gain that would make up for the scandal.

ELLEN

My freedom. Is that nothing?

ARCHER

But aren't you free already?

She looks at him.

ARCHER

It's my business to help you see these things just the way the people who are fondest of you see them, all your friends and relations. If I didn't show you honestly how they judge such questions, it wouldn't be fair of me, would it?

ELLEN

No. It wouldn't be fair.

She looks at the fire. A log breaks in two and sends up a shower of sparks.

ELLEN

Very well. I'll do as you wish.

He is a little surprised by her sudden agreement. He grabs her two hands in his.

ARCHER

I do...I do want to help you.

ELLEN

You do help me.

Archer stands up.

ELLEN

Goodnight, cousin.

Archer bends to her and KISSES her hands. She draws them away.

Cut to

INT. THEATER NIGHT

A production of a vintage play called *The Shaughraun*. We see the heavily made-up face of an ACTRESS, at the peak of a very theatrical moment, resting her arms on a mantle and bowing her face in her hands. We don't know at first that we are on stage.

CAMERA pulls out to show actor behind her. He too is very sad. This is obviously a scene of intense parting.

He moves to a door, then pauses, comes back. While the actress still has her face averted, he lifts the end of a velvet ribbon tied around her neck and kisses it.

Then he leaves and the curtain falls.

Now in CLOSE-UP: Newland Archer, watching the play. He is very moved.

As lights come up he looks around the theater. The first person he sees is Ellen Olenska, in a box with some familiar faces: Larry Lefferts and his wife, Mr. and Mrs. Beaufort, Sillerton Jackson.

CAMERA moves in on Mrs. Beaufort noticing Archer and making a languid gesture of invitation.

He rises a little reluctantly from his seat and moves out of frame.

Cut to

INT. BEAUFORT BOX/THEATER NIGHT

Everyone is chatting as ARCHER enters in the background.

LEFFERTS

It's fascinating. Every season the same play, the same scene, the same effect on the audience.

Archer is making his greetings in the box. Lefferts turns to him.

LEFFERTS

Remarkable, isn't it, Newland?

ARCHER

These actors certainly are. They're even better than the cast in London.

BEAUFORT

You see this play even when you travel? I'd travel to get away from it.

Archer seats himself just behind Ellen while

Sillerton Jackson continues to regale Regina Beaufort with details of the latest social news.

JACKSON

It was a reception at Mrs. Struthers'. Held on the Lord's day, but with champagne and singing from the tabletops. People say there was dancing.

REGINA

(a bit intrigued)
A real French Sunday, then.

Ellen turns to Archer and, inclining her head towards the stage, says in a low voice...

ELLEN

Do you think her lover will send her a box of yellow roses tomorrow morning?

ARCHER

(surprised)
I was...I was thinking about that, too. The farewell scene...

ELLEN

Yes, I know. It touches me as well.

ARCHER

Usually I leave after that scene. To take the picture away with me.

She looks down at the mother-of-pearl opera glasses in her lap.

ELLEN

I had a letter from May. From St. Augustine.

ARCHER

They always winter there. Her mother's bronchitis.

ELLEN

And what do you do while May is away?

ARCHER

(a little defensive)
I do my work.

The LIGHTS starts to go down as the audience settles in for the next act of the play. Ellen looks straight at him, WHISPERING now.

ELLEN

I do want you to know. What you advised me was right. Things can be so difficult sometimes...
(beat)
And I'm so grateful.

The curtain is up as Ellen turns quickly from Archer toward the stage, raising her opera glasses to her eyes.

As the new act begins on stage, Archer rises slowly and leaves the box.

Cut to

MONTAGE
Series of quickly DISSOLVING scenes as we hear...

NARRATOR (V.O.)
The next day, Newland Archer searched the city in vain for yellow roses.

(Director's note: camera will move always from left to right in this sequence, with images dissolving into one another, creating a circular effect.)

Shot of Archer in florist shop DISSOLVES to shot of Archer, in his office at the law firm, writing a note to Ellen.

NARRATOR (V.O.)
From his office he sent a note to Madame Olenska asking to call that afternoon and requesting a reply by messenger.

Camera tracks across note and the words "see you as soon as..."

NARRATOR (V.O.)
There was no reply that day. Or the next.

Scene DISSOLVES to street outside florist shop. Archer walks by. There are yellow roses in the window.

NARRATOR (V.O.)

And when yellow roses were again available, Archer passed them by. It was only on the third day that he heard from her, by post, from the van der Luydens' country home.

Fast cut to

EXT. COUNTRY ROAD DAY

A lovely wintery scene. Ellen Olenska, bundled in warm fur, sits in a sleigh.

CAMERA moves in as she speaks straight to it.

ELLEN

"I ran away the day after I saw you at the play, and these kind friends have taken me in. I wanted to be quiet and think things over. I feel so safe here. I wish..."

Fast cut to

INSERT

These words, in longhand, as they are in the letter. They fill the screen as she says them: "...that you were with us."

ELLEN (V.O.)

(simultaneously)

"...that you were with us."

Fast cut to

EXT. COUNTRY ROAD DAY

Ellen, still to CAMERA.

ELLEN

"Yours sincerely..."

Fast cut to

INT. LAW OFFICE DAY

Archer, with Ellen's letter in front of him, scribbling a note at the desk. CAMERA moves in on him.

NARRATOR (V.O.)

He had a still outstanding invitation from the Lefferts' for a weekend on the Hudson and he hoped it was not too late to reply. Their house was not far from the van der Luydens.

Cut to

EXT. COUNTRY ROAD DAY

A snowy landscape under bright sun. A single tree on a rise near a winding country road. In the distance, we can just make out a figure in a RED CLOAK.

Archer moves into frame in CLOSE-UP. Sees the figure far down the road. He goes out of frame and we DISSOLVE to...

...Ellen, in the red cloak, with her back to us. Archer enters frame, and she turns.

ARCHER

I came to see what you were running away from.

Cut to

EXT. COUNTRY ROAD DAY

Archer and Ellen walking.

ELLEN

I knew you'd come.

ARCHER

That shows you wanted me to.

ELLEN

Cousin May wrote she asked you to take care of me.

ARCHER

I didn't need to be asked.

ELLEN

Why? Does that mean I'm so helpless and defenseless? Or that women here are so blessed they never feel need?

ARCHER

What sort of need?

ELLEN

Please don't ask me. I don't speak your language.

They are walking past an old house with squat walls and small square windows.

ELLEN

Henry left the old Patroon house open for me. I wanted to see it.

Ellen has already started up the front stairs of the house.

Cut to

INT. PATROON HOUSE DAY

A big bed of EMBERS gleams in the kitchen chimney under a hanging iron pot. Archer throws a log on the embers, looks over to Ellen.

She sits in a rush-bottomed armchair just across the tile hearth. Her cloak is loose over her shoulders. She SMILES at him.

ARCHER

When you wrote me, you were unhappy.

ELLEN

Yes. But I can't feel unhappy when you're here.

Archer stands near a window, looking out, not quite able to look at her.

ARCHER

I can't be here long.

ELLEN

I know. But I'm a little impulsive. I live in the moment when I'm happy.

ARCHER

Ellen. If you really wanted me to come...if I'm really to help you...you must tell me what you're running from.

She does not answer. He keeps looking out the window.

Then he feels her, coming up behind him. Her arms are around his neck, HUGGING him.

He turns...and sees her as she really is, still in the chair. He looks back out the window. And now he sees...

The FIGURE of a man in a long coat with a heavy fur collar coming along the path to the house: Julius Beaufort.

ARCHER

Ah!

He laughs. Ellen moves quickly to his side.

Extreme CLOSE-UP: she slips her hand into his.

Then she looks out the window and sees Beaufort.

She steps back, startled.

ARCHER

Is he what you were running from? Or what you expected?

ELLEN

I didn't know he was here.

Archer pulls his hand from hers and walks to the front door, throwing it open. Bright SUNLIGHT rushes into the room, silhouetting Archer and Ellen, who is a few steps behind him.

ARCHER

Hello, Beaufort! This way! Madame Olenska was expecting you.

Beaufort enters with assurance, addressing his remarks to Ellen.

BEAUFORT

Well, you certainly led me a bit of a chase, making me come all this way just to tell you I'd found the perfect little house. It's not on the market yet, so you must take it at once.

There is a beat of silence, of some fleeting discomfort. Beaufort finally takes notice of Archer.

BEAUFORT

Well, Archer. Rusticating?

Archer stares back at him without answering. And Ellen looks at them both. Of the three, only Beaufort seems untroubled.

Cut to

INT. STUDY/ARCHER HOUSE NIGHT

Later. Archer is alone in his study, surrounded by books he's unpacking from a carton.

NARRATOR (V.O.)

That night he did not take the customary comfort in his monthly shipment of books from London. The taste of the usual was like cinders in his mouth, and there were moments when he felt as if he were being buried alive under his future.

Cut to

INT. BEDROOM/ELLEN'S HOUSE NIGHT

Ellen, at a writing table in the bedroom.

CAMERA moves in on her as she writes hastily.

ELLEN (V.O.)

"Newland. Come late tomorrow. I must explain to you."

Cut to

INT. STUDY/ARCHER HOUSE NIGHT

CAMERA moves in on Archer, reading Ellen's note.

He holds it in his lap, on top of an open book.

CAMERA shoots CLOSE from the side as he CRUMPLES the note and CLOSES the book. allowing a glimpse of the title: a volume of poetry by Rossetti.

Cut to

EXT. GARDEN/ST. AUGUSTINE DAY

A small figure in a WHITE DRESS in the distance, surrounded by greenery.

Archer moves into the frame in CLOSE-UP. He sees the figure across the open lawn in front of him. He goes out of frame and we DISSOLVE TO...

...May, in the white dress. Archer enters the frame.

(This scene should match Archer's meeting Ellen previously.)

May looks at him, surprised.

MAY

Newland! Has anything happened?

ARCHER

Yes. I found I had to see you.

Cut to

EXT. GARDEN/ST. AUGUSTINE DAY

CAMERA moves into tight CLOSE-UP as Archer and May sit on a garden bench. He takes her face in his hands gently and starts to KISS her.

His gentleness turns more insistent. She responds at first, but then draws back, a little startled.

ARCHER

What is it?

MAY

Nothing.

They are both a little embarrassed. She lets her hand slip out of his.

ARCHER

Tell me what you do all day.

MAY

> (brightening)
> Well, there are a few very pleasant people from Philadelphia and Baltimore who were picnicking at the inn. The Merrys are planning to lay out a lawn tennis court...

CAMERA moves in very close on Archer. May's voice fades and MUSIC comes up as he stares ahead, not listening to her litany of daily routine.

MUSIC fades and, quietly, he interrupts her.

ARCHER

> But I thought...I came here because I thought I could persuade you to break away from all that. To advance our engagement.

He reaches for her hand.

ARCHER

> Don't you understand how much I want to marry you? Why should we dream away another year?

MAY

> I'm not sure I do understand. Is it because you're not certain of still feeling the same way about me?
> Archer is on his feet.

ARCHER

> God, I...maybe...I don't know.

MAY

> Is there's someone else?

ARCHER

> Someone else? Between you and me?

MAY

> Let's talk frankly, Newland. Sometimes I've felt a difference in you, especially since our engagement.

He starts to protest. She hurries on.

MAY

> If it's untrue, then it won't hurt to talk about it. And if it's true...why shouldn't we talk about it now? You might have made a mistake.

Archer stares at the path. There is a pattern of sunny leaves beneath his feet.

ARCHER

> If I'd made some sort of mistake, would I be down here asking you to hurry our marriage?

MAY

> I don't know. You might. It would be one way to settle the question.

He sees: under the brim of her straw hat, her face TREMBLING.

MAY

> At Newport, two years ago, before we were...promised...everyone said there was...someone else for you. I even saw you sitting together with her once, I think. On a verandah, at a dance. When she came back into the house, her face was sad, and I felt sorry for her. Even after, when we were engaged, I could see how she looked.

He looks up quickly. There is a look of relief on his face which he manages to conceal at once.

ARCHER

> Is that what you've been concerned about? That's long past.

MAY

> Then is there something else?

ARCHER

> Of course not.

MAY

> (rushing on)
> Whatever it may have been, Newland, I couldn't have my happiness made out of a wrong to somebody else. We couldn't build a life on a foundation like that. If promises were made...or pledges...if you said something to the...the person we've spoken of...if you feel in some way pledged to her...and there's any way you can fulfill your pledge...even by her getting a divorce...Newland, don't give her up because of me!

Archer is beside her, holding her.

ARCHER

There are no pledges. There are no promises that matter.

May looks as if a great weight had been taken from her.

ARCHER

That is all I've been trying to say. There is no one between us, May. There is nothing between us. That is precisely my argument for marrying quickly.

She puts her arms around him. He HOLDS her close.

NARRATOR (V.O.)

He could feel her dropping back to inexpressive girlishness. Her conscience had been eased of its burden. It was wonderful, he thought, how such depths of feeling could co-exist with such an absence of imagination.

He kisses her again. But more politely.

Cut to

INT. DRAWING ROOM/MRS. MINGOTT'S HOUSE DAY

ARCHER and MRS. MINGOTT are having tea and talking.

MRS. MINGOTT

And did you succeed?

ARCHER

No. But I'd still like to be married in April. With your help.

MRS. MINGOTT

Well, you're seeing the Mingott way. When I built this house the family reacted as if I was moving to California. Now you're challenging everyone.

ARCHER

Is this really so difficult?

MRS. MINGOTT

The entire family is difficult. Not one of them wants to be different. And when they are different they end up like Ellen's parents. Nomads. Continental wanderers. Or like dear Medora, dragging Ellen about after they died, lavishing her with an expensive but incoherent education. Out of all of them, I don't believe there's one that takes after me but my little Ellen.
(smiling)
You've got a quick eye. Why in the world didn't you marry her?

Archer's taken aback momentarily. Then...

ARCHER

(laughs)
For one thing, she wasn't there to be married.

MRS. MINGOTT

No, to be sure. And she's still not. The Count, you know. He's sent a letter.

ARCHER

No, I didn't know.

MRS. MINGOTT

Mr. Letterblair says the Count wants Ellen back. On her own terms.

ARCHER

I don't believe it.

MRS. MINGOTT

The Count certainly does not defend himself. I will say that. And Ellen would be giving up a a great deal to stay here. There's her old life. Gardens at Nice with terraces of roses. Jewels, of course. Music and conversation. She says she goes unnoticed in Europe, but I know that her portrait has been painted nine times. All that, and the remorse of a guilty husband. Ellen says she cares for none of it, but still. These are things that must be weighed.

ARCHER

I would rather see her dead.

MRS. MINGOTT

(shrewdly)
Would you? Would you really? We should remember marriage is marriage. And Ellen is still a wife.

Behind Mrs. Mingott, doors open and Ellen enters, still wearing hat and cloak, her face vivid and happy. She stoops to kiss her grandmother and holds her hand out to Archer.

MRS. MINGOTT

Ellen, see who's here.

ELLEN

Yes, I know.
(to Archer)
I went to see your mother to ask where you'd gone. Since you never answered my note.

MRS. MINGOTT

Because he was in such a rush to get married, I'm sure. Fresh off the train and straight here. He wants me to use all my influence, just to marry his sweetheart sooner.

ELLEN

Well surely, Granny, between us we can persuade the Wellands to do as he wishes.

MRS. MINGOTT

There, Newland, you see. Right to the quick of the problem. Like me.
(to Ellen)
I told him he should have married you.

ELLEN

And what did he say?

MRS. MINGOTT

Oh, my darling, I leave you to find that out.

Archer, who has done his best to abide this teasing, now rises to go. As he gets to his feet, his hand TOUCHES Ellen's.

Cut to

INT. MINGOTT HOUSE/DOORWAY DAY
Ellen and Archer at the front door.

We see: extreme CLOSE-UP of their two faces close together, his mouth near her ear.

ARCHER
(quietly)
When can I see you?

Cut to

INT. HALLWAY ELLEN'S HOUSE EVENING
The SICILIAN MAID opens the door and takes Archer's coat. She hangs it quickly, then PICKS UP a large bouquet of crimson roses, with purple pansies at their base, and starts to carry them toward the drawing room.
CAMERA PANS with the MAID and the lavish bouquet as we hear...

ELLEN (O.S.)
Natasia, take those to that nice family down the street.

Archer turns his attention from the ostentatious flowers to ELLEN, who's coming down the hall toward him.

ELLEN
And come right back. The Struthers' are sending a carriage for me at seven.

She holds out her hand to Archer.

ELLEN
Who's ridiculous enough to send me a bouquet? I'm not going to a ball. And I'm not engaged.

Cut to

INT. DRAWING ROOM/ELLEN'S HOUSE NIGHT
Start on CLOSE-UP of Ellen's hand, reaching into a box for a cigarette and lighting it.

ELLEN
I'm sure Granny must have told you everything about me.

ARCHER
She did say you were used to all kinds of splendors we can't give you here.

Ellen is standing by the mantle. Archer approaches her. We see his face in the MIRROR, betraying some tangible apprehension. Behind him, on a table, is a vase full of orchids.

ELLEN
Well, I'll tell you. In almost everything she says there's something true, and something untrue. Why? What has she been telling you?

ARCHER
I think she believes you might go back to your husband.

He is standing close to her. Ellen shakes her head

ARCHER
I think she believes you might at least consider it.

ELLEN
A lot of things have been believed of me. But if she thinks I would consider it, that also means she would consider it for me. As Granny is weighing your idea of advancing the marriage.

ARCHER
(under pressure)
May and I had a frank talk in Florida. Probably our first. She wants a long engagement to give me time...

ELLEN
Time to give her up for another woman?

ARCHER
If I want to.

ELLEN
That's very noble.

ARCHER
Yes. But it's ridiculous.

ELLEN
Why? Because there is no other woman?

ARCHER
No. Because I don't mean to marry anyone else.

ELLEN
This other woman...does she love you, too?

ARCHER
There is no other woman. I mean, the per-

son May was thinking of...was never...

He sees: her hands, holding her fan.

ARCHER
(slowly)
...she guessed the truth. There is another woman. But not the one she thinks.

He sits down beside her. He takes her hands, UN-CLASPING them, so her fan falls to the floor.
She gets up and moves away from him.

ELLEN
Don't make love to me. Too many people have done that.

ARCHER
I've never made love to you. But you are the woman I would have married if it had been possible for either of us.

ELLEN
Possible? You can say that when you're the one who's made it impossible.

ARCHER
I've made it...

ELLEN
Isn't it you who made me give up divorcing? Didn't you talk to me, here in this room, about sacrifice and sparing scandal because my family was going to be your family? And I did what you asked me. For May's sake. And for yours.

She sinks down on the sofa. He stays near the mantle.

ARCHER
But there were things in your husband's letter...

ELLEN
I had nothing to fear from that letter. Absolutely nothing. You were just afraid of scandal for yourself, and for May.

He puts his face in his hands. After a moment, he goes to her. She is CRYING like a child.

ARCHER
Ellen. No. Nothing's done that can't be undone. I'm still free. You can be, too.

Now he's holding her. Her face is so close to his...He kisses her.

And she kisses him back, PASSIONATELY.
Then she breaks away.
They stare at each other. Then she shakes her head.

ARCHER

No! Everything is different. Do you see me marrying May now?

ELLEN

Would you ask her that question? Would you?

ARCHER

I have to ask her. It's too late to do anything else.

ELLEN

You say that because it's easy, not because it's true.

ARCHER

This has changed everything.

ELLEN

No. The good things can't change. All that you've done for me, Newland, that I never knew. Going to the van der Luydens because people refused to meet me. Announcing your engagement at the ball so there would be two families standing behind me instead of one. I never understood how dreadful people thought I was.

She SEES him looking at her questioningly.

ELLEN

Granny blurted it out one day. I was stupid, I never thought. New York seemed so kind and glad to see me. But there was no one as kind as you. They never knew what it meant to be tempted. But you did. You understood. You hated happiness brought by disloyalty and cruelty and indifference. I'd never known that before, and it's better than anything I've known.

She speaks in a very low voice. Suddenly he KNEELS. The TIP of her SATIN SHOE shows under her dress. He KISSES it.
She bends over him.

ELLEN

Newland. You couldn't be happy if it meant being cruel. If we act any other way I'll be making you act against what I love in you most. And I can't go back to that way of thinking. Don't you see? I can't love you unless I give you up.

Archer SPRINGS to his feet.

ARCHER

And Beaufort, with his orchids? Can you love him?
(furious)
May is ready to give me up!

With a SWEEP of his arm he sends the orchids flying into the mirror, SPILLING flowers and water everywhere. Ellen is motionless.

ELLEN

(quietly)
Three days after you pleaded with her to advance your engagement she will give you up?

ARCHER

She refused! That gives me the right...

ELLEN

The right? The same kind of ugly right as my husband claims in his letters?

ARCHER

No, of course not! But if we do this now...afterward, it will only be worse for everyone if we...

ELLEN

(almost screaming)
No, no, no!

They look at each other for a moment more. Then Ellen picks up a bell and rings for the maid.
CAMERA tilts up from spilled flowers on the floor to the face of the maid as she enters. She carries Ellen's cloak and hat, and a telegram.

ELLEN

I won't be going out tonight after all.

ARCHER

(sarcastic)

Please don't sacrifice. I have no right to keep
you from your friends.

MAID
(in Italian)
This was delivered.

She hands the WIRE to Ellen, who opens the yellow envelope, looks quickly at the message, then
hands it to Archer.

As he takes it, we...

Cut to

EXT. GARDEN/ST. AUGUSTINE DAY
May, smiling joyously, speaks in profile as CAM-
ERA MOVES IN FROM MEDIUM TO EXTREME CLOSE UP.
The light behind and around her is intense.

MAY
"Granny's telegram was successful. Papa and
Mama agreed to marriage after Easter. Only
a month!"

End on EXTREME CLOSE UP of her LIPS as she re-
cites those last three words and...
...CUT TO MAY, full-face now in MEDIUM CLOSE
UP, speaking directly to CAMERA as it MOVES QUICK-
LY in on her.

MAY
"I will telegraph Newland. I'm too happy
for words and love you dearly. Your grateful
cousin May."

CAMERA MOVES into her EYES, so CLOSE that, as
she starts to speak her name, the SCREEN WHITES OUT
as we...

Cut to

INT. DRAWING ROOM/ELLEN'S HOUSE NIGHT
Extreme CLOSE-UP of May's telegram in Newland's hand. He crumples it as if that single gesture
would annihilate the news it contains.
DISSOLVE to CLOSE-UP of his face, desolate, as another images SUPERS IN OF...

Cut to

INT. PHOTOGRAPHER'S STUDIO
...MAY'S FACE, upside down, smiling formally.
Scene widens as Archer's face dissolves to show
MAY, posing in wedding dress, as seen upside down
in the VIEWING GLASS of an old camera.

DISSOLVE TO MAY, still posing, as REFLECTED in
the brass-encased LENS of the camera.
DISSOLVE TO the PORTRAIT PHOTOGRAPHER,
working under the black hood of the camera.
DISSOLVE TO MAY, POSING in the deliberately artificial setting of the photo studio. CAMERA PULLS
BACK to reveal the photo studio, then the camera,
then the photographer working behind it, and, finally, Archer, waiting at the back of the studio, watching.

NARRATOR (V.O.)
There had been wild rumors, right up to the
wedding day, that Mrs. Mingott would actually attend the ceremony. It was known
that she had sent a carpenter to measure the
front pew in case it might be altered to ac-
commodate her. But this idea, like the great
lady herself, proved to be unwieldy, and she
settled for giving the wedding breakfast.

Cut to

INSERT
CAMERA moving down a lavish array of wedding
gifts: silver bowls and exquisite china and heavy
place settings.

NARRATOR (V.O.)
The Countess Olenska sent her regrets—she
was traveling with an aunt—but gave the
bride and groom an exquisite piece of old
lace. Two elderly aunts in Rhinebeck offered
a honeymoon cottage, and, since it was
thought "very English" to have a country-
house on loan, their offer was accepted.
When the house proved suddenly uninhab-
itable, however, Henry van der Luyden
stepped in to offer an old cottage on his
property nearby.

Cut to

INSERT
CAMERA moves in on picture of the Patroon
house, where Ellen and Archer had spoken.

NARRATOR (V.O.)
May accepted the offer as a surprise for her
husband. She had never seen the house, but
her cousin Ellen had mentioned it once. She
had said it was the only house in America

where she could imagine being perfectly happy.

From picture of the house. ...

Dissolve to

INSERT

...old postcards of London: 19th century streets filled with carriages; regal figures in high hats and long dresses enjoying Sunday in Hyde Park; Bond Street crowded with shoppers.

NARRATOR (V.O.)

They traveled to the expected places, which May had never seen. In London, Archer ordered his clothes, and they went to the National Gallery, and sometimes to the theater.

Cut to

INT. CARRIAGE/STREET NIGHT

May is close to Archer on the seat, holding his arm. She has a new attitude of easy intimacy with him.

MAY

I hope I don't look ridiculous. I've never

dined out in London.

ARCHER

Englishwomen dress just like everybody else in the evening, don't they?

MAY

How can you even ask that, when they're always at the theater in old ball-dresses and bare heads.

ARCHER

Well perhaps they save their new dresses for home.

MAY

Then I shouldn't have worn this?

ARCHER

No. You look very fine.
(meaning it)
Quite beautiful.

She smiles...and surprises him with a kiss. He is DELIGHTED. She pulls away and hugs his arm.

INSERT

Old postcards of Paris: Rue Rivoli and the Rue de la Paix, glittering like jewels strung across a city; the Place de la Concorde, busy with traffic and regal even at midday.

NARRATOR (V.O.)

In Paris, she ordered her clothes. There were trunks of dresses from Worth. They visited the Tuileries.

Cut to

INT. SCULPTOR'S STUDIO DAY

ARCHER watches as the sculptor Rochée models May's folded hands in marble. May looks up at her husband and smiles.

NARRATOR (V.O.)

Rochée modeled May's hands in marble. And occasionally they dined out.

Cut to

INT. DINING ROOM/ PARIS HOUSE NIGHT

Cut to

A small formal dinner. May holding her own nicely, charming everyone.

CAMERA moves in fast on Archer. He is in conversation with a fine-boned man whose face is distinguished by a carefully nurtured mustache.

NARRATOR (V.O.)

Archer had gradually reverted to his old inherited ideas about marriage. It was less trouble to conform with tradition.

Archer glances away from his dinner companion to look across the table at the animated May.

NARRATOR (V.O.)

There was no use trying to emancipate a wife who hadn't the dimmest notion that she was not free.

Cut to

INT. CARRIAGE/STREET NIGHT

Archer and May riding home from the dinner.

ARCHER

We had an awfully good talk. Interesting fellow. We talked about books and things. I asked him to dinner.

MAY

The Frenchman? I didn't have much chance to talk to him, but wasn't he a little common?

ARCHER

Common? I thought he was clever.

MAY

I suppose I shouldn't have known if he was clever.

ARCHER

(quietly, resigned)
Then I won't ask him to dine.

NARRATOR (V.O.)

With a chill he knew that, in future, many problems would be solved for him in this same way.

Cut to

EXT. STREET/PARIS NIGHT

As their carriage moves away down a boulevard of flickering lamps.

NARRATOR (V.O.)

The first six months of marriage were usually said to be the hardest, and after that, he thought, they would have pretty nearly finished polishing down all the rough edges. But May's pressure was already wearing down the very roughness he most wanted to keep.

Cut to

EXT. STREET/PARIS NIGHT

DISSOLVE into the same street, later. It is still and empty, near dawn. The streetlamps flicker off in the light of the new day.

NARRATOR (V.O.)

As for the madness with Madame Olenska, Archer trained himself to remember it as the last of his discarded experiments. She remained in his memory simply as the most plaintive...

The last flame goes out..

NARRATOR (V.O.)

...and poignant of a line of ghosts.

On the word "ghosts," we...

Cut to

EXT. BEAUFORT LAWN/NEWPORT DAY
...a close burst of blazing WHITE.

White of summer dresses and crisp suits, punctuating the GREEN of rolling lawns by the seaside under a bright afternoon sun.

Newport, Rhode Island, a year and a half later. The spacious lawn of the Beaufort summer "cottage."

CAMERA tracks parallel to a row of men and women standing against a tent, looking out at something we can't yet see. Their summer clothes are splendid.

CAMERA continues tracking until it comes to a break in the row: the raised flap of a tent. May walks INTO FRAME, wearing a white dress with a pale green ribbon around her tiny waist and a wreath of ivy on her hat. As she walks past the row of people, she comes toward CAMERA into big CLOSE-UP and we DISSOLVE to...

May, slowly raising a bow and arrow, taking careful aim, letting go. Her movements have a classic grace.

The crowd applauds appreciatively at her shot, and at her form. We see a banner announcing "Newport Archery Club/August meeting," and, in the distance, more spectators on the verandah of the Beaufort cottage. A small white DOG dashes across the lawn, pulling its owner by a leash.

Two of the spectators are Larry Lefferts and Julius Beaufort, who watch May admiringly. Beaufort has his customary orchid fixed to the lapel of his jacket.

LEFFERTS

She's very deft.

BEAUFORT

Yes. But that's the only kind of target she'll ever hit.

Now we see: Archer, a little in front of them. He

REACTS angrily to Beaufort's remark, but says nothing.

Across the lawn, May makes her final bull's-eye. Archer starts across to join her.

May, flushed and calm, is receiving a winner's PIN from a club official as a photographer snaps her picture.

She looks up as Archer approaches. They smile at each other.

NARRATOR (V.O.)

No one could ever be jealous of May's triumphs. She managed to give the feeling that she would have been just as serene without them.

May takes Archer's arm and they walk across the lawn together. They come toward CAMERA in possible SLOW MOTION.

NARRATOR (V.O.)

But what if all her calm, her niceness, were just a negation, a curtain dropped in front of an emptiness? Archer felt he had never yet lifted that curtain.

Cut to

EXT. NARRAGANSET AVENUE/NEWPORT DAY

May and Archer in an open carriage. May handles the reins of the ponies expertly.

MAY

Has Regina Beaufort been here at all this summer?

ARCHER

I don't know. There's a great deal of gossip. I expect Beaufort will bring Annie Ring here any day.

MAY

Not even he would dare that!

ARCHER

He's reckless in everything. Even his railway speculations are turning bad. But he just answers every rumor with a fresh extravagance.

MAY

I heard he gave Regina pearls worth half a million.

ARCHER

He had no choice.

Cut to

INT. MINGOTT HOUSE/NEWPORT DAY

CAMERA close on the pin May won in the archery contest: an arrow with a diamond tip, pinned to the front of her linen blouse.

A stout hand runs fingers along the contour of the arrow and we hear the voice of...

MRS. MINGOTT

Quite stunning. It's Julius Beaufort who donates the club's prizes, isn't it. This looks like him. Of course. And it will make quite an heirloom, my dear. You should leave it to your eldest daughter.

May blushes and Mrs. Mingott pinches her arm teasingly. We are in the sun-dappled drawing room of the Mingott Newport cottage. There is a tea service on a table in front of Mrs. Mingott; the summer heat is not treating her kindly. She fans herself continuously.

MRS. MINGOTT

What's the matter, aren't there going to be any daughters? Only boys? What, can't I say that either? Look at her, blushing!

Archer laughs. Mrs. Mingott smiles and calls out...

MRS. MINGOTT

Ellen! Ellen, are you upstairs?

CAMERA close now on Archer, startled at the name.

MRS. MINGOTT

She's over from Portsmouth, spending the day with me. It's such a nuisance. She just won't stay in Newport, insists on putting up with those...what's their name...Blenkers. But I gave up arguing with young people about fifty years ago...Ellen!

A maid appears.

MAID

I'm sorry, ma'am, Miss Ellen's not in the house.

MRS. MINGOTT
She's left?

MAID
I saw her going down the shore path.
Mrs. Mingott turns to Archer.

MRS. MINGOTT
Run down and fetch her, like a good grand-
son. May can tell me all the gossip about
Julius Beaufort.

CAMERA close on Archer.

MRS. MINGOTT
Go ahead. I know she'll want to see you
both.

Cut to

EXT. SHORE PATH/NEWPORT DAY
The path descends from the bank where the
Mingott house is perched to a walk above the water.
Weeping willows are planted on both sides of the
walk. Through their branches the Lime Rock LIGHT-
HOUSE is visible.

Archer walks slowly down the path, as if moving
toward a fate he thought was past him.

NARRATOR (V.O.)
He had heard her name often enough during the year and a half since they had last
met. He was even familiar with the main in-
cidents of her life. But he heard all these ac-
counts with detachment, as if listening to
reminiscences of someone long dead.

The willow-lined walk curves toward the sea,
where there is a small wooden pier ending in a pago-
da-like summer house.

NARRATOR (V.O.)
But the past had come again into the present, as in those newly discovered caverns in
Tuscany, where children had lit bunches of
straw and seen old images staring from the
wall.

Bright SUNSET. The sun splinters in a thousand
pieces. Archer rounds the corner of the path, and sees
the pier and house in front of him. Then he sees: a
WOMAN, back to the shore, leaning against a rail. He
stops, unable to go on. It's ELLEN.

She looks out to sea, at the bay furrowed with
yachts and sailboats and fishing craft.
He does not move. Ellen does not turn.
A SAILBOAT glides through the channel between
Lime Rock lighthouse and the shore.
Still she has not turned.
Archer looks from Ellen to the sailboat, and back
again.

NARRATOR (V.O.)
He gave himself a single chance. She must
turn before the sailboat crosses the Lime
Rock light. Then he would go to her.

He looks to the boat. It glides out on the reced-
ing tide between the lighthouse and the shore.
He looks at Ellen: she seems to be drawn into the
sunset.
Back to the boat: it PASSES the lighthouse. Water
SPARKLES between its stern and the last reef of the is-
land.
Back to Ellen. She has not turned.
Archer walks away.
As he goes, we can still see Ellen's figure in the
distance. She does not turn.

Cut to

EXT. MINGOTT HOUSE/ NEWPORT DUSK
Archer and May leave the house and walk toward
their waiting carriage.

MAY
I'm sorry you didn't find her. But I've heard
she's so changed.

ARCHER
Changed?

MAY
So indifferent to her old friends. Summering
in Portsmouth, moving to Washington.
Sometimes I think we've always bored her.
I wonder if she wouldn't be happier with her
husband after all.

ARCHER
(laughs)
I don't think I've ever heard you be cruel before.

Archer helps her into the carriage.

MAY

    Cruel?

ARCHER

    Even demons don't think people are happi-
er in hell.

MAY

    (placidly)
    Then she shouldn't have married abroad.
    She starts to take the reins of the carriage. Archer
lifts them from her.

ARCHER

    Let me.

He reaches over and, in SLIGHT SLOW MOTION,
takes the REINS from her hands as they start away
from the house.

                       Cut to

INT. WELLAND HOUSE/NEWPORT MORNING

The dining room: the family is having breakfast.
Mrs. Archer and Janey are at the table, as is Mrs.
Welland. May presides over the gathering with prac-
ticed ease. The morning breeze gently lofts the long
curtains. CAMERA makes CIRCULAR TRACK around
table as it PANS with the conversation.

MRS. WELLAND

    The Blenkers. A party for the Blenkers?

JANEY

    Who are they?

MAY

    The Portsmouth people, I think. The ones
Countess Olenska is staying with.

MRS. ARCHER

    "Professor and Mrs. Emerson Sillerton re-
quest the pleasure...Wednesday afternoon
club...at 3 o'clock punctually. To meet Mrs.
and the Misses Blenker. Red Gables, Catherine Street."

She looks around the table.

MRS. ARCHER

    I don't think we can decline.

JANEY

    I don't see why, really. He's an archaeologist

and he lives here even in winter. He's always
taking his poor wife to tombs in the Yu-
catan instead of to Paris. He's got a house full
of long-haired men and short-haired wom-
en, and...

MRS. ARCHER

    And he is Sillerton Jackson's cousin.

JANEY

    (chastened)
    Of course.

MRS. WELLAND

    Some of us will have to go.

MAY

    I'll go over. And, Janey, why don't you come
with me. I'm sure Cousin Ellen will be there.
It will give you a chance to see her.
    (to Archer)
    Newland, you can find some way to spend
the afternoon, can't you?

ARCHER

    Oh I think for a change I'll just save it in-
stead of spending it.

He takes the last bite of griddle cakes left on his
plate.

ARCHER

    Maybe drive to the farm to see about a new
horse for the brougham.

                       Cut to

EXT. COUNTRY ROAD/NEWPORT DAY

Archer at the reins of the carriage. The day is
clear, the sky a brilliant ultramarine.

He leans a little way out of the carriage to check
a name posted at the front of the lane, then turns the
horses in.

We see the name on the post: Blenker.

                       Cut to

EXT. DRIVE/BLENKER HOUSE/NEWPORT DAY

In the near distance, an ill-kept house with peel-
ing white paint.

Closer: a shed for horses. Archer stops and ties up
his team.

Empty and quiet. The click of locusts in the still
air. Archer looks toward the house, sees...

...to its left, a ghostly summer house of trellis-work that had once been white.

He walks toward the summer house.

As he gets closer, he sees a box garden, and something pink just beyond it.

DISSOLVE to tight shot: a pink PARASOL, inside the summer house.

DISSOLVE to Archer's face, staring at it, almost hypnotized. He walks toward the CAMERA. As he blocks it we...

...DISSOLVE again to the parasol. Close on it as Archer's hand enters the frame to pick it up. CAMERA moves in on his face as he lifts the handle close to him. It is carved of rare wood. He smells its scent.

And lifts the handle closer...slowly...to his lips.

SOUND: of soft skirts behind him. We see: Archer's eyes, in huge CLOSE-UP, closing in anticipation.

CAMERA pulls out as he waits for Ellen's touch. But he hears only a voice behind him...

KATIE BLENKER
Hello?

His eyes open. He turns and sees...

...Katie Blenker, an adolescent girl with open, friendly curiosity. She looks, for an instant, familiar: Archer thinks that he has been surprised by May.

KATIE BLENKER
I'm sorry, did you ring, I've been asleep in the hammock...

ARCHER
I didn't mean to disturb you. Are you Miss Blenker? I'm Newland Archer.

KATIE
I've heard so much about you.

ARCHER
I came up the island to see about a new horse, and I thought I'd call. But the house seemed empty...

KATIE
It is empty. They're all at the party. The one the Sillertons are giving for us. Didn't you know?

He keeps looking at her, not knowing what to say.

KATIE
Everyone's there but me, with my fever, and Countess Olenska...oh, you found my parasol!

She takes it from his hand.

KATIE
It's my best one. It's from the Cameroons.

ARCHER
(trying to be casual)
The Countess was called away?

KATIE
A telegram came from Boston. She said she might be gone for two days. I do love the way she does her hair, don't you? It reminds me of Sir Walter Scott.

CAMERA moves close on Archer. He is struggling with himself.

ARCHER
(interrupting her)
You don't know...I'm sorry...I've got to be in Boston tomorrow. You wouldn't know where she was staying?

Cut to

EXT. BOSTON COMMON DAY
A sweltering summer day.

CAMERA close on an oil PAINTING of the park scene. It nicely captures the trees and flowers under shimmering heat, the summer colors of suits and dresses...and the figure of a woman, seated mid-perspective, on a bench, reading a volume of poetry.

DISSOLVE to an even tighter shot of the woman in the painting. A BRUSH works on her features.

DISSOLVE to Archer, watching the painter. He turns, squinting into the glare of the morning sun at the woman seated a little way in front of him on the bench.

FAST PAN over to her. It is Ellen.

Cut to

EXT. BOSTON COMMON DAY
Ellen looks up. Archer is beside her.

ELLEN

(startled)

Oh.

(now smiling)

Oh.

Without rising, she makes room for him on the bench. He sits beside her and tries making casual conversation.

ARCHER

I'm here on business. Just got here, actually.

He stares at her. Being casual is too difficult.

ARCHER

You're doing your hair differently.

ELLEN

Only because the maid's not with me. She stayed back in Portsmouth. I'm only here for two days, it didn't seem worth...

ARCHER

You're traveling alone?

ELLEN

(sly)

Yes. Why, do you think it's a little dangerous?

ARCHER

(smiling)

Well, it's unconventional.

ELLEN

I suppose it is. I hadn't thought of it. I've just done something so much more unconventional. I've refused to take back money that belonged to me.

ARCHER

Someone came with an offer?

She nods.

ARCHER

What were the conditions?

ELLEN

(simply)

I refused.

ARCHER

(pressing)

Tell me the conditions.

ELLEN

Nothing unbearable, really. Just to sit at the head of his table now and then.

Archer chooses his words carefully.

ARCHER

And he wants you back, at any price?

ELLEN

Well, it's a considerable price. At least it's considerable for me.

ARCHER

So you came to meet him.

She stares, then laughs suddenly.

ELLEN

My husband? Here? No, of course not. He sent someone.

ARCHER

(very careful now)

His secretary?

ELLEN

Yes. He's still here, in fact. He insisted on waiting. In case I changed my mind.

He is trying to absorb all this.

ELLEN

They told you at the hotel I was here?

He nods, but still says nothing. After a moment...

ELLEN

You haven't changed, Newland.

Now he looks straight into her eyes.

ARCHER

(intense)

I had changed, till I saw you again.

ELLEN

Please don't.

ARCHER

Just give me the day. I'll say anything you

like. Or nothing. I won't speak unless you
tell me to. All I want is some time with you.
All I want is to listen to you.
He is so intense Ellen has to look away from
him. She takes out a small gold-faced watch
on an enamel chain.

ARCHER

    I want to get you away from that man. Was
    he coming to the hotel?

ELLEN

    At eleven. Just in case...

ARCHER

    Then we must leave now. It's been a hun-
    dred years since we've met.

ELLEN

    Where will we go?

ARCHER

    Where?

He's stumped: emotion has gotten in the way of
foresight. He seems addled for a moment. She smiles
at him.

ELLEN

    Somewhere cool, at any rate.

ARCHER

    We'll take the steamboat down to Point Ar-
    ley. There's an inn.

ELLEN

    I'll have to leave a note at the hotel.
    He pulls a note-case from his pocket, fum-
    bling a little.

ARCHER

    Write it here. I have the paper...you see how
    everything's predestined?...and this...have
    you seen these...the new stylographic pen...

He hands her the case and pulls out a fountain
pen.

ARCHER

    Just steady the case on your knee, and I'll get
    the pen going in a second...

He bangs the hand holding the pen against the

back of the bench.

ARCHER

    It's like jerking down the mercury in a ther-
    mometer. Now try.

He hands her the pen and she starts to write a
name on an envelope. EXTREME CLOSE UP, from in
front: of her HAND, with the pen, beginning to write
a name, "Riv..."

                       Match cut to
EXT. PARKER HOUSE HOTEL/BOSTON DAY
The envelope, sealed now, with a name we can't
read.

ARCHER

    Shall I take it in?

ELLEN

    I'll only be a moment.

She disappears through the glazed doors of the
hotel.
    An Irish woman walks by, selling peaches. Archer
declines.
    The door of the hotel opens. He turns. A group
of men comes onto the sidewalk and walks away.
Archer watches them with mild interest.
    He hears the doors again and looks over. A MAN,
dressed in a distinctly European fashion and looking
a little worried, appears on the sidewalk. He looks
around, but does not seem to notice Archer.
    Archer sees him, however. Something about his
face is familiar, but Archer can't quite place it...
    ...and the man is off, down the street.
    SOUND of the hotel doors again. He turns, and
Ellen is at his side.

                           Cut to

INT./EXT. INN DAY
(POSSIBLE start on MATTE SHOT of white clap-
board inn situated on a bluff overlooking the Atlantic, with a ferry boat coming toward it.)
    We see out the window of the inn: the BILLOW-
ING WHITE SAIL of a small boat. CAMERA pulls back
to reveal...
    ...a long wooden verandah overlooking a gentle
lawn and the Atlantic. Archer and Ellen sit at a table
covered with a checkered cloth held down from the
ocean breezes by a bottle of pickles at one end and a

blueberry pie under a clear dish at the other. SOUNDS of a party in the large dining room of the inn occasionally interrupt the stillness.

Ellen looks at the distant sailboat, then turns to Archer.

ELLEN

Why didn't you come down to the beach to get me the day I was at Granny's?

ARCHER

Because you didn't turn around. You didn't know I was there. I swore I wouldn't call you unless you looked around.

ELLEN

But I didn't look around on purpose.

ARCHER

You knew?

ELLEN

I recognized the carriage when you drove in. So I went to the beach.

ARCHER

To get as far away from me as you could.

ELLEN

As I could. Yes.

ARCHER

Well you see, then. It's no use. It's better to face each other.

ELLEN

I only want to be honest with you.

ARCHER

Honest? Isn't that why you always admired Julius Beaufort? He was more honest than the rest of us, wasn't he? We've got no character, no color, no variety. I wonder why you just don't go back to Europe.

ELLEN

I believe it's because of you.

ARCHER

Me? I'm the man who married one woman because another one told him to.

ELLEN

You promised not to say those things today.

ARCHER

I can't keep that promise.

ELLEN

And what about May? What does May feel? That's the thing we've always got to think of, by your own showing.

ARCHER

My showing?

ELLEN

Yes, yours. Otherwise everything you taught me would be a sham.

ARCHER

If you're using my marriage as some victory of ours, then there's no reason on earth why you shouldn't go back.

(looking right at her)

You gave me my first glimpse of a real life. Then you asked me to go on with the false one. No one can endure that.

ELLEN

I'm enduring it.

He looks at her.

ARCHER

You too? All this time, you too?

She does not reply.

ARCHER

What's the use? We can't be like this. When will you go back?

ELLEN

I won't. Not yet. Not as long as we both can stand it.

ARCHER

This is not a life for you.

ELLEN

It is. As long as it's part of yours.

ARCHER

And the way I live...my life...how can it be part of yours?

She looks away. He reaches for her hands, holds them.

ELLEN

Don't...don't be unhappy.

ARCHER

You won't go back? You won't go back?

ELLEN

I won't go back.

She lets go of his hands, turns and STANDS.
DISSOLVE TO Ellen, moments later, leaving the room. Archer remains seated.
DISSOLVE TO Archer, standing and following her out.
DISSOLVE TO the EMPTY ROOM.

Cut to

EXT. STREET/NEW YORK AUTUMN DAY
EXTREME LONG LENS SHOT of BROADWAY. SCREEN is FILLED with MEN, ARCHER among them, all coming towards us on their way to work, and all wearing the same derby.
CUT TO sidewalk just outside Archer's law offices. The day is stifling, and a HOT WIND BLOWS from both rivers. Men clutch their derbies to their heads.
Archer turns into the entrance of his office building as a man steps toward him. He is the SAME MAN

Archer glimpsed outside the Parker House in Boston.

RIVIERE

(French accent)
It's Mr. Archer, I think?

ARCHER

Yes?

In the background, as the men speak, several women walk by, holding their skirts down and their hats close.

RIVIERE

My name is Riviere. We dined together in Paris last year.

ARCHER

Oh yes. I'm sorry I didn't quite recall....
And we should remember, as Archer does now, the face of the man with the fine mustache we first encountered during the Paris montage.
People mill around them like rushing water as they stand talking.

RIVIERE

Quite alright. I had the advantage. I saw you yesterday in Boston.

Archer is taken aback by this.

Cut to

INT. ARCHER'S OFFICE DAY

The window is closed because of the hot autumn wind, and heat has settled on the room like a curse. Occasional street NOISE, of pedestrians and carriage traffic, underscores the conversation. Riviere seems slightly uncomfortable, but handles himself impeccably. Both men perspire.

ARCHER

I still do not understand why we're speaking.

RIVIERE

I came here on Count Olenska's behalf because I believed...in all good faith...that it would be best for the Countess to return to him. I met her in Boston and told her all the Count had said. She did me the kindness of listening carefully. But she's changed, Monsieur.

ARCHER

(a tinge of jealous suspicion)
You knew her before?

RIVIERE

I used to see her in her husband's house. The Count would never have trusted my mission to a stranger.

ARCHER

This change...

RIVIERE

It may only have been my seeing her for the first time as she is. As an American. And if you're an American of her kind...of your kind...

CAMERA starts to move in on Archer.

RIVIERE

...things that are accepted in certain other societies, or at least put up with for the sake of...convenience...these things become intolerable. She made her marriage in good faith. It was a faith that the Count could not share, and could not understand. So her faith was shattered. And it was only coming back here...coming home...that restored it. Returning to Europe would mean a life of some comfort. And considerable sacrifice. And also, I would think, no hope.

Archer looks at his presidential calendar hanging on the wall, then down at the papers scattered on his mahogany desk.

He hears a SOUND—of a chair moving back, of Riviere getting to his feet—and he looks up. Riviere is standing in front of the desk.

RIVIERE

I will fulfill my obligation to the Count and meet with the family. I will tell them what he wishes and suggests for the Countess. But I ask you, Monsieur, to use your own influence with them. I...I beg you...with all the force I'm capable of...not to let her go back.

Archer looks at him with astonishment. Riviere's eyes fix momentarily on Archer, then look around the room. Archer extends his hand.

ARCHER

Thank you.

Cut to

INT. DINING ROOM/MRS. ARCHER'S HOUSE EVENING

A traditional Thanksgiving affair attended by Janey and Mrs. Archer, Newland and May, Mrs. Welland and Sillerton Jackson.

Start on MEDIUM CLOSE UP of turkey being carved on the sideboard.

MRS. ARCHER (O.S.)

Well, Boston is more conservative than New York. But I always think it's a safe rule for a lady to lay aside her French dresses for one season.

DISSOLVE TO MEDIUM CLOSE UP of sliced turkey being served.

MRS. ARCHER (O.S.)

When Old Mrs. Baxter Pennilow died, they found her standing order—forty-eight Worth dresses—still wrapped in tissue paper.

DISSOLVE TO MEDIUM CLOSE UP of cranberry sauce in a crystal serving dish.

MRS. ARCHER (O.S.)

When her daughters left off their mourning they wore the first lot to the Symphony without looking in advance of the fashion.

DISSOLVE TO CAMERA TRACKING DOWN TABLE beside a servant. Mrs. Archer continues talking as CAMERA moves away.

NARRATOR (V.O.)

He had written to her once in Washington. Just a few lines, asking when they were to meet again. And she wrote back: "Not yet."

CAMERA, MOVING SLIGHTLY CLOSER, STOPS on Archer's distracted face just on those last two words. He barely notices the servant offering cranberry sauce.

JANEY

I think it was Julius Beaufort who started the new fashion by making his wife clap her new clothes on her back as soon as they arrived. I must say, it takes all Regina's distinction not to look like...

JACKSON

(helpfully)
Her rivals?

JANEY

...like that Annie Ring.

MRS. ARCHER

Careful, dear.

JANEY

Well, everybody knows.

JACKSON

Indeed. Beaufort always put his business around. And now that his business is gone there are bound to be disclosures.

MAY

Gone? Is it that bad?

JACKSON

As bad as anything I've ever heard of. Most everybody we know will be hit, one way or another.

CAMERA DOLLIES IN on Jackson, ending in a MEDIUM CLOSE UP as he speaks the last words.

Cut to

INT. LIBRARY/ARCHER HOUSE NIGHT
Archer and Jackson stand in front of a painting in the Gothic library. Archer helps Jackson light a cigar.

JACKSON

(walking away to sit down)
Very difficult for Regina, of course. And it's a pity...it's certainly a pity...that Countess Olenska refused her husband's offer.

ARCHER

Why, for God's sake?

JACKSON

Well...to put it on the lowest ground.... what's she going to live on now?

ARCHER

Now...?

Archer moves to sit down next to Jackson.

JACKSON

Well, I mean now that Beaufort...

ARCHER

What the hell does that mean, sir?

JACKSON

(continuing tranquilly)
Most of her money's invested with Beaufort, and the allowance she's been getting from the family is so cut back...

ARCHER

She has something, I'm sure.

JACKSON

Oh I would think a little. Whatever remains after sustaining Medora. But I know the family paid close attention to Monsieur Riviere and considered the Count's offer very closely. Everyone hopes the Countess herself might simply see that living here, on such a small margin...

ARCHER

If everyone would rather she be Beaufort's

mistress than some decent fellow's wife, you've all gone about it perfectly.

ARCHER bangs his BRANDY SNIFTER on the table and remains standing. Jackson looks at him attentively.

ARCHER
She won't go back.

JACKSON
That's your opinion, eh? Well no doubt you know. I suppose she might still soften Catherine Mingott, who could give her any allowance she chooses. But the rest of the family has no particular interest in keeping Madame Olenska here. They'll simply let her find her own level.

Archer sees: a cone of ASH dropping from Jackson's cigar into a brass tray at his elbow.

ARCHER
(pause)
Shall we go up and join my mother?

Cut to

INT. ARCHER HOUSE HALLWAY NIGHT
As May and Archer arrive home from Thanksgiving. Servants take their coats.

Cut to

INT. ARCHER HOUSE NIGHT
Archer and May climb the staircase to the second floor of their house. The LAMP May holds throws deep long SHADOWS on the wall.

ARCHER
The lamp is smoking again. The servants should see to it.

MAY
I'm sorry.

He stops at the door of his study. She stops and bends over to lower the wick. The light shines on her shoulders and the curve of her face.

ARCHER
I may have to go to Washington for a few days.

MAY
When?

ARCHER
Tomorrow. I'm sorry, I should have said something before.

MAY
On business?

ARCHER
On business, of course. There's a patent case coming up before the Supreme Court. I just got the papers from Letterblair. It seems...

MAY
Never mind. I'm sure it's too complicated. I have enough trouble managing this lamp.

He helps her with the wick.

MAY
But the change will do you good.
The flame is stronger now.

MAY
And you must be sure to go and see Ellen.

He looks at her in the newly bright lamp light. Does she know? He thinks she might.

Cut to

INT. ARCHER HOUSE NIGHT
CAMERA close on a note being carried quickly on a silver tray through the hall.
WIDER to show: a maid, carrying the note to Archer and May.

ARCHER MAID
Excuse me, ma'm. But this came while you were out.

May reaches for the note.

ARCHER
(indicating lamp)
Do something about this, will you, Agnes?

He indicates the lamp, which still smokes slightly. The maid nods, gives him her old lamp and takes the faulty one away.
May looks up from the note.

MAY
Granny's had a stroke.

Cut to

INT. BEDROOM, HALLWAY, AND DRAWING ROOM/MINGOTT HOUSE MORNING

Start on low angle of servants' FEET, walking slowly and with difficulty...as if supporting some great weight. Mrs. Mingott's elegantly slippered feet occupy the center of the frame.

MRS. MINGOTT

A stroke! I told them all it was just an excess of Thanksgiving.

CAMERA PULLS OUT and TILTS UP from low angle to reveal Mrs. Mingott being carried by several servants in a heavy CHAIR out of her bedroom as if she were some potentate from the subcontinent. They move through the hall and into the drawing room. Aside from breathing a bit more heavily, the old woman seems little the worse for wear, although her speech is a trifle slurred. May and Archer walk beside her.

MRS. MINGOTT

Dr. Bencomb acted most concerned and insisted on notifying everyone as if it were the reading of my last testament. But I won't be treated like a corpse when I'm hardly an invalid.

The servants are having some difficulty managing the chair at the entrance to the drawing room. Archer steps in to help out and prevent Mrs. Mingott from tipping out onto the floor.

MRS. MINGOTT

You're very dear to come. But perhaps you only wanted to see what I'd left you.

MAY

Granny, that's shocking!

Archer and the servants set Mrs. Mingott down as CAMERA MOVES in for EXTREME CLOSE UP. She is in the drawing room, in her accustomed spot.

MRS. MINGOTT

It was shock that did this to me. It's all due to Regina Beaufort. She came here last night, and she asked me...

As she talks, we SEE what Archer IMAGINES...

Cut to

EXT. MINGOTT HOUSE NIGHT

The door opens and CAMERA moves in on the face of Regina Beaufort. She wears a thick veil, and looks, for a moment, like a figure from a Gothic novel.

MRS. MINGOTT (V.O.)

...she had the effrontery to ask me...to back Julius. Not to desert him, she said. To stand behind our common lineage in the Townsend family.

Cut to

INT. DRAWING ROOM/MINGOTT HOUSE NIGHT

The regal Regina Beaufort, dressed in black as if for mourning, speaking animatedly to an intractable Mrs. Mingott.

MRS. MINGOTT (V.O.)

I said to her, "Honor's always been honor, and honesty's always been honesty, in Manson Mingott's house, and will be 'till I'm carried out feet first." And then...if you can believe it...she said to me...

CAMERA close on the tearful face of Regina Beaufort.

MRS. MINGOTT (V.O.)

..."But my name, Auntie. My name's Regina Townsend." And I said, "Your name was Beaufort when he covered you with jewels, and it's got to stay Beaufort now that he's covered you with shame."

Cut to

INT. DRAWING ROOM/MINGOTT HOUSE DAY

Mrs. Mingott finishes her story.

MRS. MINGOTT

So I gave out. Simply gave out. Now family

will be arriving from all over expecting a funeral and they'll have to be entertained. I don't know how many notes Bencomb sent out.

ARCHER

If there's any way we can help...

MRS. MINGOTT

Well my Ellen is coming. I expressly asked for her. She arrives this afternoon on the train. If you could fetch her...

ARCHER

Of course. If May will send the brougham, I can take the ferry.

MAY

(the slightest pause)
There, you see, Granny. Everyone will be settled.

Cut to

INT./EXT. CARRIAGE DAY

CAMERA STARTS high overhead and MOVES IN as Archer and May leave Mrs. Mingott's house and enter their carriage.

MAY

I didn't want to worry Granny. But how can you meet Ellen and bring her back here if you have to go to Washington yourself this afternoon.

ARCHER

I'm not going. The case is off. Postponed. I heard from Letterblair this morning.

MAY

Postponed? How odd. Mama had a note from him this morning as well. He was concerned about Granny but he had to be away. He was arguing a big patent case before the Supreme Court. You said it was a patent case, didn't you?

ARCHER

Well, that's it. The whole office can't go. Letterblair decided to go this morning.

CAMERA now holds them both in VERY TIGHT TWO SHOT.

MAY

Then it's not postponed?

The blood rises in Archer's face.

ARCHER

No. But my going is.

May looks away from him. CARRIAGE MOVES
FORWARD and brings Archer into a SINGLE TIGHT
CLOSE UP before carrying him out of frame.

Cut to

EXT. TRAIN STATION DAY

Close DISSOLVE onto a swarm of passengers disembarking in EXTREME SLOW MOTION from a steam
train that we can only see in outline. The passengers
walk toward the camera like ghosts from the past.

NARRATOR (V.O.)

He knew it was two hours by ferry and carriage from the Pennsylvania terminus in Jer-
sey City back to Mrs. Mingott's.

We see: Archer's face, searching the crowd for
Ellen.

NARRATOR (V.O.)

All of two hours. And maybe a little more.

DISSOLVE to CLOSE UPS of passengers as they walk
through the steam, still in EXTREME SLOW MOTION
and INTERCUT with CLOSE UPS of feet disembarking
down the train's steel steps.

DISSOLVE from a final face to ELLEN'S FACE, in the
crowd.

As CAMERA MOVES BACK, and Archer is already
at her side. He motions for the porter carrying her
bags to follow them, then draws her arm through his.

ARCHER

You didn't expect me today?

ELLEN

No.

ARCHER

It was Granny Mingott who sent me. She's
much better. I nearly went to Washington to
see you. We would have missed each other.

They are at the carriage. CAMERA PULLS BACK
NOW to show other travelers all around them: the
faces of the recently wealthy, the poor and the
newly emerging middle class. This is the only time
that we glimpse a suggestion of a world outside
the rigid borders of society. As all these travelers
swarm around them, Archer helps Ellen into the
carriage.

Cut to

INT. CARRIAGE DAY

DISSOLVE quickly into Ellen seated in the carriage, Archer sitting close beside her.

ARCHER

Did you know...I hardly remembered you.

ELLEN

Hardly remembered?

ARCHER

I mean...I mean it's always the same. Each
time I see you. You happen to me all over
again.

ELLEN

Oh yes. I know, I know. For me too.

She puts her hand in his. The carriage starts to
move.

Quick series of close DISSOLVES: he bends over. He
UNBUTTONS her tight brown glove. He KISSES the
palm of her hand. She turns her hand over and CA-
RESSES his cheek.

Cut to

INT. CARRIAGE DUSK

Later on in the journey to Mrs. Mingott's. Ellen
and Archer sit very close in the cab. A WIND blows
outside.

ARCHER

Your husband's secretary came to see me.
The day after we met in Boston.

She seems surprised.

ARCHER

You didn't know?

ELLEN

No. But he told me he had met you. In Paris,
I think.

ARCHER

Ellen...I have to ask you. Just one thing.

ELLEN

Yes?

ARCHER

Was it Riviere who helped you get away after you left your husband?

ELLEN

Yes. I owe him a great debt.

ARCHER

(quietly)
I think you're the most honest woman I ever met.

ELLEN

(slight smile)
No. But probably one of the least fussy.

ARCHER

Ellen, we can't stay like this. It can't last.

ELLEN

What?

ARCHER

Our being together and not being together. It's impossible.

ELLEN

You shouldn't have come today.

Suddenly she turns to him and flings her arms around him, pressing him CLOSE, kissing him passionately. He returns all her feeling.

The LIGHT from a gas lamp on the street flashes in through the window and makes her draw away, suddenly silent and motionless, to the corner of the carriage.

ARCHER

Don't be afraid. Look, I'm not even trying to touch your sleeve. Being like this isn't what I want. I need you with me. I can even just sit still, like this, and look at you.

ELLEN

I think we should look at reality, not dreams.

ARCHER

(desperate)
I just want us to be together.

ELLEN

I can't be your wife, Newland. Is it your idea I should live with you as your mistress?

ARCHER

I want...somehow I want to get away with you. Find a world where words like that won't exist.

ELLEN

Oh my dear...where is that country? Have you ever been there? Is there anywhere we can be happy behind the backs of people who trust us?

ARCHER

I'm beyond caring about that.

ELLEN

No you're not! You've never been beyond that. I have. I know what it looks like. A lie in every silence. It's no place for us.

He looks at her, dazed. Then he reaches for the small cab bell that signals orders to the coachman. The coach pulls up. Archer starts out.

ELLEN

Why are we stopping? This isn't Granny's.

ARCHER

No. I'll get out here.
He steps down to the street.

ARCHER

You were right. I shouldn't have come today.
He closes the door.

Cut to

EXT. STREET DUSK
Archer signals and the coach pulls away.

The wind blows stronger. Archer holds his hat and touches his eyes. There are TEARS.
He turns and walks away down the street.

Cut to

INT. LIBRARY/ARCHER HOUSE NIGHT

Start on CLOSE UP of Japanese print. CUT TO Archer, looking at the print in a beautiful leather-bound book, which is now in lower left of frame.

May is embroidering a sofa cushion. Firelight casts a strong glow in the room.

Archer looks up from his book, SEES: May's arms, as she works the needle. The sleeves of her dress have slipped back. Her sapphire betrothal ring shines on her left hand above her wedding band.

May sees him looking at her, smiles.

MAY

What are you reading?

ARCHER

Oh, a history. About Japan.

MAY

Why?

ARCHER

I don't know. Because it's a different country.

MAY

You used to read poetry. It was so nice when you read it to me.

He gets to his feet.

ARCHER

I need some air.

He goes to the window, opens it, leans out into the cold.

MAY

Newland! You'll catch your death.

ARCHER

Catch my death. Of course.

He turns, shuts the window, looks at May, who has gone back to her embroidery.

NARRATOR (V.O.)

But then he realized, I am dead. I've been dead for months and months.

CAMERA moves closer on him, watching May.

NARRATOR (V.O.)

Then it occurred to him that she might die.

People did. Young people, healthy people, did. She might die, and set him free.

May sees him looking at her.

MAY

Newland?

He walks to her and touches her head.

ARCHER

Poor May.

MAY

Poor? Why poor?

ARCHER

Because I'll never be able to open a window without worrying you.

MAY

I'll never worry if you're happy.

ARCHER

And I'll never be happy unless I can open the windows.

MAY

In this weather?

Cut to

EXT. STREET/ELLEN'S HOUSE NIGHT

Light SNOW. Ellen comes down the front steps of her house toward a carriage that waits for her at the curb.

As she approaches the carriage door, Archer steps out of the shadows.

ARCHER

I have to see you. I didn't know when you were leaving again.

ELLEN

I'm due at Regina Beaufort's. Granny lent me her carriage.

ARCHER

With all that's happened, you're still going to see Regina Beaufort?

ELLEN

I know. Granny says Julius Beaufort is a scoundrel. But so is my husband, and the family still wants me to go back to him.

Two FIGURES, illuminated by the glowing street lamps but still a little indistinct in the blowing snow, are walking down the street toward Ellen and Archer.

ARCHER
But you won't go back?

ELLEN
No. Granny's asked me to stay and help care for her. But I think it's me she means to help. She said I've lived too long locked up in a cage. She's even seen to my allowance.

The two figures draw nearer, then discretely cross to the other side of the street. As they pass under the streetlight we recognize one of the two men: LARRY LEFFERTS.

Archer and Ellen see them and draw a little closer to the sheltering shadow of the carriage.

ARCHER
You won't need my help if you have Granny's.

ELLEN
I will still need your help. If I stay, we will have to help each other.

ARCHER
I have to see you. Somewhere we can be alone.

ELLEN
(smiles)
In New York?

ARCHER
Alone. Somewhere we can be alone. There's the art museum in the park. Half past two tomorrow. I'll be at the door.

She nods and takes his arm. He helps her quickly into the carriage.
We SEE: her gloved hand gliding off his.

Cut to

INT. ART MUSEUM DAY
A obscure gallery in the brand new Metropolitan Museum.
CAMERA starts close on Ellen's eyes, behind the mesh of a veil.

DISSOLVE TO a case full of beautiful pre-Roman antiquities with REFLECTIONS of sarcophagi or larger sculpture in the glass. The ancient objects are in the foreground; in the background, clearly visible, are the faces of Archer and Ellen, studying the objects.

DISSOLVE TO a small, delicate piece of sculpture with a legend underneath on a handwritten museum card: "Use Unknown."

DISSOLVE to Archer and Ellen, sitting on a divan near a heating system in the center of the room. Through the far door is a diminishing perspective of other galleries.

Even though they are alone in the room, they both speak softly. Their WHISPERS are sibilant in these marble walls.

ARCHER
You came to New York because you were afraid.

ELLEN
Afraid?

ARCHER
Of my coming to Washington.

ELLEN
I promised Granny to stay in her house because I thought I would be safer.

ARCHER
Safer from me?

She bends her head.

ARCHER
Safer from loving me?

EXTREME CLOSE-UP. What Archer sees: a tear, hanging in the mesh of her veil.

ELLEN
(pause)
Shall I come to you once, and then go home?

He doesn't answer. She gets up and starts out. He CATCHES her by the arm.

ARCHER
Come to me once, then.

They look at each other almost like enemies.

ARCHER
(pressing)
When? Tomorrow?

ELLEN
(hesitating)
The day after.

She moves away down the long gallery. He follows her.

ELLEN
No. Don't come any farther than this.

She hurries to the gallery door, turns, then leaves.
DISSOLVE from her, small in the distance, framed in the gallery door, to...

Cut to

INT. LIBRARY/ARCHER HOUSE NIGHT
Archer is at his desk. An envelope addressed to Ellen is near him; his pen is poised over a piece of vellum on which he is writing an address for their rendezvous. A KEY, to go with the address, is ready to be sealed in the envelope as he looks up, slightly startled...
...as May enters, a little agitated.

MAY
I'm sorry I'm late. You weren't worried, were you?

He SWEEPS the key, envelope and addresss into his desk drawer before she is near enough to notice.

ARCHER
Is it late?

She removes her velvet hat as she speaks, drawing the long hatpins from her glistening hair.

MAY
Past seven. I stayed at Granny's because Cousin Ellen came in.

Archer reacts to the mention of Ellen's name. May doesn't seem to notice.

MAY
We had a wonderful talk. She was so dear. Just like the old Ellen. And Granny's so charmed by her.

He listens to this, still beguiled by her apparent kindness.

MAY
You do see, though, why sometimes the family has been annoyed? Going to see Regina Beaufort in Granny's carriage...

Now he gets up, annoyed at the same old prattle.

ARCHER
Aren't we dining out?

He starts past her, and she moves forward, almost impulsively. She throws her arms around him and presses her cheek to his.

MAY
You haven't kissed me today.

She is trembling.

Cut to

INT. THEATER NIGHT
CAMERA looks down on May from above. She is sitting serenely in a theater box. She wears a beautiful dress of blue-white satin and old lace.
CAMERA moves in slowly to her as we hear...

NARRATOR (V.O.)
It was the custom, in old New York, for brides to appear in their wedding dress during the first year or two of marriage. But May, since returning from Europe, had not worn her bridal satin until this evening.

On those last words, we quickly see...
CAMERA close on a bright bunch of DAISIES; petals being sprinkled on the ground.
MUSIC up: it is the yearly performance of *Faust*. A woman starts to sing an aria.
In a reprise of the opening scene, we DISSOLVE to the face of Newland Archer, who is surveying the audience from the back of the club box. CAMERA PANS (his POV) as he looks across the row of boxes, sees: May, in her wedding dress.
Then he looks over to the Mingott box, where he first saw Ellen Olenska. It is empty.

Cut to

INT. THEATER NIGHT
As in the opening scene: Archer's POV as he

151

walks quickly down the theater corridor, past its red velvet walls.

Cut to

INT. THEATER NIGHT

CAMERA on Archer, tight, as he enters box and leans over to May.

ARCHER

My head's bursting. Don't tell anyone, but please come home with me.

May looks at him, then whispers to her mother. Mrs. Welland whispers an excuse to her companion, Mrs. van der Luyden, as May rises and leaves with her husband.

As she goes, she puts her hand on his.

Cut to

INT. LIBRARY/ARCHER HOUSE NIGHT

Starting with CAMERA close on Archer's hand as he opens a silver box and takes out a cigarette.

CAMERA pans with cigarette, as we hear...

MAY

Shouldn't you rest?

Archer walks to the fireplace, May near him.

ARCHER

My head's not as bad as that. And there's something important I have to tell you right away.

May sits down in an armchair, looking at him expectantly. Archer's library is newly decorated with dark embossed paper, Eastlake bookcases and writing table.

ARCHER

May...There's something I've got to tell you....about myself....

May sits still. Her face is tranquil, but very pale.

ARCHER

Madame Olenska...

MAY

(interrupting)
Oh, why should we talk about Ellen tonight?

ARCHER

Because I should have spoken before.

MAY

Is it really worthwhile, dear? I know I've been unfair to her at times. Perhaps we all have. You've understood her better than any of us, I suppose. But does it matter, now that it's all over?

ARCHER

Over? How do you mean, over?

MAY

Why, since she's going back to Europe so soon.

Archer's hand grips the corner of the mantelpiece.

MAY

Granny approves and understands. She's disappointed, of course, but she's arranged to make Ellen financially independent of the Count. I thought you would have heard today at your offices.

He stares, not really seeing her. She lowers her eyes.

Silence.

A lump of coal falls forward in the grate. May gets up to push it back and Archer turns to face her.

ARCHER

It's impossible.

MAY

Impossible? Certainly she could have stayed here, with Granny's extra money. But I guess she's given us up after all.

ARCHER

How do you know that?

MAY

From Ellen. I told you I saw her at Granny's yesterday.

ARCHER

And she told you yesterday?

152

MAY

No. She sent me a note this afternoon. Do
you want to see it?

May moves to the desk and pulls the note from a
small pile of mail on the desk.

MAY

I thought you knew.

She holds out a note. He moves to her and takes it.
As CAMERA MOVES IN very close on Archer now,
the LIGHTING in the room seems to FADE. There are
SHADOWS like slanted bands across his face.

ELLEN (V.O.)

"May dear, I have at last made Granny understand that my visit to her could be no
more than a visit, and she has been as kind
and generous as ever. She sees now that if I
return to Europe I must live by myself. I am
hurrying back to Washington to pack up,

and I sail next week. You must be very good
to Granny when I'm gone...as good as you've
always been to me."

We see Archer's head now in CLOSE UP. His EYES,
reading the note, are ILLUMINATED by a single strip
of LIGHT.

ELLEN (V.O.)

"If any of my friends wish to urge me to
change my mind, please tell them it would
be utterly useless."

LIGHT in the room COMES UP as Archer looks
away from the note to May.

ARCHER

Why did she write this?

MAY

I suppose because we talked things over yesterday.

ARCHER

What things?

MAY

I told her I was afraid I hadn't been fair to
her. I hadn't always understood how hard it
must have been here.

Archer is struggling hard to keep himself together.

MAY

I knew you'd be the one friend she could always count on. And I wanted her to know
that you and I were the same. In all our feelings.
(more slowly)
She understood why I wanted to tell her this.
I think she understands everything.

She takes one of his cold hands and presses it
quickly to her cheek.

MAY

My head aches, too. Good night, dear.

She turns and walks toward the door. Her wedding dress makes a soft SOUND in the still room.

Cut to

INT. DINING ROOM/ARCHER HOUSE NIGHT
CAMERA moves down the long dining room
table, seeing: openwork silver baskets, containing
Maillard bonbons, placed between candelabra; a lavish centerpiece of Jacqueminot roses and maidenhair;
the finest china and silver; hand-written dinner
menus edged in gold.

NARRATOR (V.O.)

It was, as Mrs. Archer said to Mrs. Welland,
a great event for a young couple to give their
first dinner, and it was not to be undertaken
lightly. There was a hired chef, two bor-
rowed footmen, roses from Henderson's,
Roman punch and menus on gilt-edged

154

cards. It was considered a particular triumph that the van der Luydens, at May's request, stayed in the city to be present at her farewell dinner for the Countess Olenska.

Big CLOSE-UP of Archer. He goes through the motions of eating, but he has the face of a man in suspended animation.

CAMERA MOVES slowly out from him. First we see who's seated on Archer's left: Ellen, wearing several rows of amber beads around her neck.

NARRATOR (V.O.)
Archer saw all the harmless-looking people at the table as a band of quiet conspirators, with himself, and Ellen, the center of their conspiracy.

Gradually shot widens to include the room: there is a piano in a corner with a large basket of flowers.

NARRATOR (V.O.)
He guessed himself to have been, for months, the center of countless silently observing eyes and patiently listening ears. He understood that, somehow, the separation between himself and the partner of his guilt had been achieved. And he knew that now the whole tribe had rallied around his wife.

CAMERA (crane) ends on overhead shot of room: about twenty GUESTS—including Mrs. Welland and Mrs. Archer, Janey and the van der Luydens and the Leffertses and the Jacksons—are enjoying the dinner and making easy conversation.

NARRATOR (V.O.)
He was a prisoner in the center of an armed camp.

Now we see: CLOSE-UP of Archer's dazed and troubled face. Table chatter continues. We hear, over...

JANEY
Regina's not well at all, but that doesn't stop Beaufort from devoting as much time to Annie Ring...

As conversation drones on, CAMERA tilts down toward Archer's coat pocket, and we DISSOLVE...
...through his coat...

...inside his pocket...
...to a sealed envelope, with his name and address on the outside...
...through this envelope...
...to a SECOND ENVELOPE, the one which Archer addressed to Ellen...
...through this envelope to the vellum, with their rendezvous address...
...and the key, lying beside the address in the folded note.

Now CUT back to CLOSE-UP of Archer. PULL OUT to TWO SHOT with Ellen sitting next to him. In an act of will, he turns to her.

ARCHER
Was the trip from Washington very tiring?

ELLEN
The heat in the train was dreadful. But all travel has its hardships.

ARCHER
Whatever they may be, they're worth it. Just to get away.

She can't reply.

ARCHER
I mean to do a lot of traveling myself soon.

Ellen's face trembles. To rescue the moment, he leans toward a man sitting across from him.

ARCHER
Philip, what about you? A little adventure? A long trip? Are you interested? Athens and Smyrna and maybe Constantinople. Then as far East as we can go.

PHILIP
Possibly, possibly.

MRS. VAN DER LUYDEN
But not Naples. Dr. Bencomb says there's a fever.

ARCHER
There's India, too.

PHILIP
You must have three weeks to do India properly.

INT. LIBRARY/ARCHER HOUSE NIGHT

After dinner. The men are gathered in several groups, all smoking cigars. Archer still seems to be disengaged from everything happening around him, even though he manages to maintain appearances.

CAMERA starts close on group of several men near Archer

LEFFERTS

Beaufort may not receive invitations anymore, but it's clear he still maintains a certain position.

PHILIP

Horizontal, from all I've heard.

CAMERA moves out to include others in group: Larry Lefferts, van der Luyden, Sillerton Jackson.

LEFFERTS

(indignant)
If things go on like this, we'll be seeing our children fighting for invitations to swindlers' houses and marrying Beaufort's bastards.

JACKSON

Has he got any?
Laughter from the group.

GUEST

Careful, there, gentlemen. Draw it mild, draw it mild.

Archer manages a small smile, but is still distracted. He starts to walk straight toward the CAMERA.

CAMERA pans with him as he goes. Van der Luyden comes to his side (from left side of frame) and gently takes his elbow. We see, in TWO-SHOT: van der Luyden, in profile, as he speaks to Archer. Archer's back is turned.

VAN DER LUYDEN

Have you ever noticed? It's the people who have the worst cooks who are always yelling about being poisoned when they dine out. Lefferts used to be a little more adept, I thought. But then, grace is not always required. As long as one knows the steps.

As van der Luyden speaks, the dialogue FADES and CAMERA moves in on Archer, back still turned to us, lost in his own thoughts. We end on tight CLOSE-UP of the back of Archer's head. Behind him, the wall SHIFTS COLOR (to a deep lavender or dark red) as we...

Cut to

INT. HALLWAY/ARCHER HOUSE NIGHT

CAMERA in tight CLOSE-UP of Archer's face. PULL BACK to see: Archer, standing in the doorway of the drawing room. Over his shoulder, we see other men coming down from the library to join the ladies.

PAN from Archer slowly across room. We see May, sitting on a gilt sofa next to Countess Olenska. May looks over, sees Archer. Her eyes are shining as she gets up.

As soon as she's on her feet, Mrs. van der Luyden beckons Ellen to join her across the room.

Mrs. van der Luyden is standing next to a tall period PORTRAIT displayed on an easel. Having the painting situated in the room this way makes the subject of the portrait, a woman in formal dress, seem almost to be living, another party guest. Ellen comes slowly toward Mrs. van der Luyden, and another woman joins them.

CAMERA pans with all this careful social choreography. Archer watches the ritual as if it were an elaborate rehearsal for a firing squad. We hear...

NARRATOR (V.O.)

The silent organization which held this whole small world together was determined to put itself on record. It had never for a moment questioned the propriety of Madame Olenska's conduct. It had never questioned Archer's fidelity. And it had never heard of, suspected, or even conceived possible, anything at all to the contrary.

CAMERA pans across the roomful of guests chatting with languid animation.

NARRATOR (V.O.)

From the seamless performance of this ritual, Archer knew that New York believed him to be Madame Olenska's lover.

CAMERA now on May.

NARRATOR (V.O.)
And he understood, for the first time, that his wife shared the belief.

May looks at him and smiles.

Cut to

INT. FRONT HALL/ARCHER HOUSE NIGHT
CAMERA (Archer's POV) swoops down on Ellen's bare shoulders in a great desperate rush.

Archer is helping her on with her cloak. Other guests are leaving. A sharp wind comes through the open door, making the candlelight in the hallway flicker.

ARCHER
Shall I see you to your carriage?

She turns to him as Mrs. van der Luyden, swathed in sable, steps forward.

MRS. VAN DER LUYDEN
(casual)
We are driving dear Ellen home.

Ellen, grasping her fan of eagle feathers and holding her cloak closed, offers her hand to Archer.

ELLEN
Good-bye.

ARCHER
Good-bye. But I'll see you soon in Paris.

ELLEN
Oh...if you and May could come...

Mr. van der Luyden comes forward to offer his arm. She takes it, and walks down the steps of the house.
Archer watches from the doorway. He sees:
Ellen, stepping into the carriage. For a moment, as she gets herself settled, he can see her FACE in the dim streetlight.
Then she sits back, and she is LOST in shadow.

Cut to

INT. UPPER HALLWAY/ARCHER HOUSE NIGHT
May, holding a lamp, climbs the stairs of the now silent house. Archer is a few steps behind her.
He stops, and goes toward the open door of the library.
May keeps going.

Cut to

INT. LIBRARY/ARCHER HOUSE NIGHT
Archer looks lost in the room. May, pale but still full of energy after the long night, now appears in the doorway.

MAY
It did go off beautifully, didn't it.

ARCHER
Oh. Yes.

MAY
May I come in and talk it over?

ARCHER
Of course. But you must be very sleepy.

MAY
No. I'm not. I'd like to be with you a little.

ARCHER
Fine.

They sit in separate chairs near the fire.

ARCHER
(pause)
Since you're not tired and want to talk, there's something I have to tell you. I tried the other night.

MAY
Oh yes, dear. Something about yourself?

ARCHER
About myself, yes. You say you're not tired. But I am. I'm tired of everything. I want to make a break...

MAY
You mean give up the law?

ARCHER
Well, maybe. To get away, at any rate. Right away. On a long trip. Go somewhere that's so far...

MAY
How far?

ARCHER
I don't know. I thought of India. Or Japan.

She stands up and walks toward him.

MAY

 As far as that? But I'm afraid you can't, dear...
(unsteady voice)
...not unless you take me with you. That is, if
the doctors will let me go...but I'm afraid
they won't.

He stares at her, his eyes nearly wild.

MAY

 I've been sure of something since this morning and I've been longing to tell you...

She sinks down in front of him, puts her face
against his knee.

ARCHER

 Oh.

He strokes her hair with his cold hand.

MAY

 You didn't guess?

ARCHER

 No. Of course, I mean, I hoped, but...

He looks away from her.

ARCHER

 (quietly)
Have you told anyone else?

MAY

 Only Mama, and your mother.
(a beat)

And Ellen. You know I told you we'd had a long
talk one afternoon...and how wonderful she was to
me.

ARCHER

 Ah.

MAY

 Did you mind my telling her, Newland?

ARCHER

 Mind? Why should I? But that was two
weeks ago, wasn't it? I thought you said you
weren't sure till today.

MAY

 (face flushed)
No. I wasn't sure then. But I told her I was.
And you see...

She looks up at him, moving closer.

MAY

 I was right.

She is very close to him now, expecting to be
kissed. Her eyes are wet with VICTORY.
CAMERA close on Newland. He's speechless. He
averts his eyes.
CAMERA follows his desperate gaze around the
room. It starts to PAN slowly. After several moments
we hear...

NARRATOR (V.O.)

 It was the room in which most of the real
things of his life had happened.

CAMERA continues to PAN slowly around the
room, from left to right.

NARRATOR (V.O.)

 Their eldest boy, Theodore, too delicate to

be taken to church in midwinter, had been christened there.

DISSOLVE to another PAN, moving in the same direction: a baby being christened by an Episcopal bishop. May, Archer and the rest of the family standing by, proud and pleased.

DISSOLVE to PAN continuing slowly across room. We begin to notice gradual changes: in the furniture; in the furnishings; in the lighting.

NARRATOR (V.O.)

It was here that Ted took his first steps. And it was here that Archer and his wife always discussed the future of all their children. Bill's interest in archeology. Mary's passion for sport and philanthropy. Ted's inclinations toward "art" that led to a job with an architect, as well as some considerable redecoration.

CAMERA pans slowly past a Chippendale cabinet

and some English mezzotints.

DISSOLVE to PAN in same direction, tighter than the one before: of Mary, a stalwart young girl, being embraced by a happy, older May.

NARRATOR (V.O.)

It was in this room that Mary had announced her engagement to the dullest and most reliable of Larry Lefferts' many sons. And it was in this room, too, that her father had kissed her through her wedding veil before they motored to Grace Church.

DISSOLVE to PAN in same direction, very tight: of Archer kissing his daughter through the veil.

DISSOLVE to continuing PAN of the library.

NARRATOR (V.O.)

He was a dutiful, loving father, and a faithful husband. When May died of infectious pneumonia after nursing Bill safely through, he had honestly mourned her. The world of

her youth had fallen into pieces and rebuilt itself without her ever noticing.

CAMERA has completed pan of room, and now moves slowly in on a silver-framed picture of the young May, dressed in her Newport Archery costume.

NARRATOR (V.O.)

This hard bright blindness, her incapacity to recognize change, made her children conceal their views from her, just as Archer concealed his. She died thinking the world a good place, full of loving and harmonious households like her own.

CAMERA is close on the picture, which rests on Archer's Eastlake writing-table. Near it: a shaded electric lamp. And the marble model of May's folded hands that was done in Paris during their honeymoon.

NARRATOR (V.O.)

Newland Archer, in his fifty-seventh year, mourned his past and honored it.

We hear, for the first time: a SOUND that is both startling and familiar....the RINGING of a telephone.
CAMERA PANS to phone, and to Archer's hand picking up the receiver.
CAMERA follows the phone and reveals his face: at 57, he shows the evidence of a full life behind him.

ARCHER

Yes? Hello?

OPERATOR (V.O.)

Chicago wants you.

TED (V.O.)

Dad?

ARCHER

Ted?

TED (V.O.)

I'm just about finished out here, but my client wants me to look at some gardens before I start designing.

ARCHER

Fine. Where?

TED (V.O.)

Europe. I'll have to sail next Wednesday, on the *Mauretania.*

ARCHER

And miss the wedding?

TED (V.O.)

Annie will wait for me. I'll be back on the first and our wedding's not 'till the fifth.

CAMERA starts to PAN around the room again. We hear the rest of this conversation while seeing the other side of the changed room.

ARCHER

(affectionate)
I'm surprised you remember the date.

TED (V.O.)

Well, I was hoping you'd join me. I'll need you to remind me of what's important. What do you say? It will be our last father and son trip.

ARCHER

I appreciate the invitation, but...

TED (V.O.)

Wonderful. Can you call the Cunard office first thing tomorrow

CAMERA has come to rest on the window. Through the softly blowing curtains we see: a sunny street on a fine New York spring day.

And we..

Dissolve to

INT. BRISTOL HOTEL ROOM/PARIS DAY
Another window. Now the city is Paris, the street outside the Faubourg St. Honore. The spring day is equally fine.
CAMERA PANS around room, left-to-right. The luxurious furnishings make a distinct contrast to Archer's darker, subtler library. END on Archer, sitting on a divan near the window, looking out.

A hand comes in and touches his shoulder. He turns: it's Ted. He has his mother's bearing. But he has Archer's eyes.

TED

I'm going out to Versailles with Tourneur. Will you join us?

ARCHER

I thought I'd go to the Louvre.

TED

I'll meet you there later, then. Countess Olenska is expecting us at half-past five.

ARCHER

(stunned)
What?

TED

Oh, didn't I tell you. Annie made me swear to do three things in Paris. Get her the score of the last Debussy songs. Go to the Grand Guignol. And see Madame Olenska. You know she was awfully good to Annie when Mr. Beaufort sent her over to the Sorbonne.

CAMERA moves close on Archer as his son talks, until only Archer is in the frame. We see, in his face, signs of memories flooding back.

TED

Wasn't the Countess friendly with Mr. Beaufort's first wife or something? I think Mrs. Beaufort said that she was. In any case, I called the Countess this morning and introduced myself as her cousin and...

ARCHER

You told her I was here?

TED

Of course. Why not? She sounds lovely. Was she?

ARCHER

Lovely? I don't know. She was different.

Cut to

INSERT

A series of paintings of the Italian Renaissance,

DISSOLVING quickly from one to another.

NARRATOR (V.O.)

Whenever he thought of Ellen Olenska, it had been abstractly, serenely, like an imaginary loved one in a book or picture. She had become the complete vision of all that he had missed.

Last painting of the short series is a Titian of almost palpable sensuality.
HOLD on this as we hear...

ARCHER (V.O.)

(whispering)
But I'm only fifty-seven.

And we...

Dissolve to

INT. LOUVRE/PARIS DAY

Archer's face, melancholy and uncertain now, studying the Titian.
Dazzles of afternoon light flood the gallery. He turns and walks away.

Cut to

EXT. TUILERIES/PARIS AFTERNOON

Ted and Archer, deep in conversation, walk through the great gardens on their way to Madame Olenska's.

TED

Did Mr. Beaufort really have such a bad time of it, when he wanted to remarry? No one wanted to give him an inch.

ARCHER

Perhaps because he had already taken so much.

TED

As if anyone remembers any more. Or cares.

ARCHER

Well, he and Annie Ring did have a lovely daughter. You're very lucky.

TED

We're very lucky, you mean.

ARCHER

Yes, that's what I mean.

TED

So considering how that all turned out...and considering all the time that's gone by...I don't see how you can resist.

ARCHER

Well, I did have some resistance at first to your marriage, I've told you that...

TED

No, I mean resist seeing the woman you almost threw everything over for. Only you didn't.

ARCHER

(cautious)
I didn't.

TED

No. But mother said...

ARCHER

Your mother?

TED

Yes. The day before she died. She asked to see me alone, remember? She said she knew we were safe with you, and always would be. Because once, when she asked you to, you gave up the thing you wanted most.

Archer walks on in silence for a few moments.

ARCHER

She never asked me.

                                    Cut to

EXT. RUE DU BAC/PARIS DAY

A quiet quarter off a busy boulevard. Archer stands in a little square, looking up at a contemporary building with balconies running up its cream-colored front.

CAMERA (Archer's POV) MOVES across the surface of the building.

NARRATOR (V.O.)

After a little while he did not regret Ted's in-

discretion. It seemed to take an iron band from his heart to know that, after all, someone had guessed and pitied...And that it should have been his wife moved him inexpressibly.

Ted crosses the square to his father.

TED

The porter says it's the fifth floor.

He casually slips his arm through his father's.

TED

It must be the one with the awnings.

They both look toward an upper balcony, just above the horse-chestnut trees in the square. The day is fading into a soft sun-shot haze. The sun makes reflections on the window.
Ted turns to his father.

TED

It's nearly six.

Archer sees an empty bench under a tree.

ARCHER

I think I'll sit a moment.

TED

Do you mean you won't come?

Archer shrugs.

TED

You really won't come at all?

ARCHER

I don't know.

TED

She won't understand.

ARCHER

Go on, son. Maybe I'll follow you.

He walks toward the bench, Ted following him.

TED

But what will I tell her?

ARCHER

(as he sits)
Don't you always have something to say?

TED

I'll tell her you're old-fashioned and you insist on walking up five flights instead of taking the elevator.

ARCHER

(pause)
Just say I'm old-fashioned. That should be enough.

Ted gives his father a look of affectionate exasperation, then crosses the square and goes into the building.
Archer sits on the bench, watching him go.
Then he LOOKS UP at the windows on the fifth floor.
The setting sun makes dazzling REFLECTIONS on the glass.
A CURTAIN moves, briefly, then falls back into place.
The sun suddenly makes a bright FLARE on the pane, stinging Archer's eyes. He moves his head slightly and we...

Cut to

EXT. SUMMER HOUSE/NEWPORT DUSK
Another sunset, almost thirty years before.
A SAILBOAT starts to sail between the shore and a LIGHTHOUSE.
Ellen, in the summer house, watches it. Her back is to us.
The sailboat glides between the shore and the lighthouse. The SUN dances on the water.
Ellen stands in the last brilliant burst of the setting sun. She starts to move.
She TURNS AROUND.
And looks full at us, CAMERA close.
And SHE SMILES.

Dissolve to

EXT. RUE DU BAC/PARIS DAY
DISSOLVE onto balcony window. A servant starts to roll up the awning.
WIDE SHOT of Archer, still on the bench, watching the awning being secured. The servant finishes, goes back inside.
Archer remains on the bench, alone in the twilight.

FADE OUT

Sources

Edith Wharton herself appears never to have entered a movie theater.

—*R. W. B. Lewis*, Edith Wharton: A Biography

At some point soon after shooting, with the editing not half done, Marty and I had one of our frequent weekend dinners. Over the years, these casual occasions had taken on their own agenda: catch up and decompress; swap stories; plan projects and trade memories; worry about whether we should have dessert. As the years went on, we found ourselves reminiscing more and more, keeping the memories immediate and alive and making sure no dust settled over the common ground.

This dinner, this time, was a little different. We both made an effort not to mention, directly or by inference, all the *Age* work still at hand. We tried not to mention the movie at all, but of course we couldn't do it. The movie kept coming up. Never directly, though; not at first.

We never spoke of a single editing intricacy, or structural problem. Instead, as we usually do, we started to talk about movies, in a loose, freely-associative way, closing quickly onto specific titles, talking about scenes, shots, performances, quirks of story, bits of production arcana. Somewhere around the third or fourth title, Marty looked up from his plate of chow fun and hooked me with one of those half-amused, half-skeptical looks I'd come to know well. He was on to something, and was waiting for the me to catch up and catch on.

Seeking to avoid being cast as Watson to my friend's perpetual Holmes, I rattled on, praising *The Strange Affair of Uncle Harry,* a Robert Siodmak movie I'd just seen again after many years, until Marty said, "I didn't think we'd talk about *The Age of Innocence.*"

There was no getting around it, never mind getting away from it. Each of the movies we'd spoken of up till that point had some bearing on *The Age of Innocence:* as an inspiration, as a source of stylistic or spiritual nourishment, even as a temporary tool. We were used to striking sparks from unexpected places—Marty had solved a thorny blocking problem in *Age* while we watched Robert Hamer's *Pink String and Sealing Wax*—but we had not realized, till that night at dinner, just how wide a net we had cast in our Wharton adaptation.

Since this present book is an album of how influences become a confluence, we thought it might be interesting to pass along a few of the movies that, by mutual reckoning, found their way, one way or another, into *The Age of Innocence.* For us, anyway, it seems like a good time to try. Midpoint in the journey to a fixed, finished film, we find ourselves in a small clearing, still deep in the woods, looking all around, getting oriented by trying to figure how we got here in the first place.

This is how, as best we can work it out. This isn't a true filmography; it's a trail of celluloid breadcrumbs. But lurking wicked wolves, please take note: we're not putting ourselves up for membership in this company. These are simply movies that we admire, like and, in some cases, love; movies that, we reckon, somehow shaped and intrigued us. They are all part of *The Age of Innocence,* ghosts in the halls of the rambling house we've tenanted for a while.

This list does not reflect anything formal or definitive, either. Once we decided to include it in this book at all—a decision reached after realizing that, despite whatever we say, any one of these movies could and might be used to give us a reproving rap on the knuckles—we wanted to find a format that was as informal as possible. So, with some alphabetical ordering, general tinkering and the addition of the first person for me and the conventional but convenient third-person for Marty, this is a rough retrospective of our dinner conversation that evening. The requests for more chow fun and abject inquiries about dessert have been omitted.

We covered 22 titles. We might have overlooked as many more, and may have continued, too, except that there was still a movie to see that night: *London Town,* sometimes known as *My Heart Goes Crazy,* directed by Wesley Ruggles in 1946. I hope that will find its way onto another list, another time, for another film. Maybe, too, that's why we keep watching movies. To keep making them. Or, as Marty says, "to be inspired to make them. Or to be inspired to *try* and make them. Because nothing's automatic anymore, and the trying's the hardest."

That's pretty much what we tell anyone who asks why we see so many movies. We just say we're working. We keep the fun part to ourselves.

Nobody's fooled.

BARRY LYNDON (1975; color)

Director-Writer: Stanley Kubrick.

Candles. Narration. The slow zooms in and out that keep the audience just where Kubrick wants them: on the outside, as if admiring a landscape. Or—on the zoom in—closer and closer to the hard heart of this bleakly comic, ironic rake's progress. The Calvary of a simple man undone by fate, his own impetuosity, and a recognizably pragmatic set of values. Far from *Age* in theme, but not, perhaps, in tone: the chill, bemused irony of the narration—the lavish but careful use of the novelist's language—turns the drama gradually from shrewd observation of 18th-century English mores into a complex, poignant portrait of vanity and ambition. We even wrote some wild lines for Michael Gough in *Age* that recounted an incident from *Barry Lyndon* about death at a gaming club. They made for slightly racier conversation than usual at a formal dinner in 1870s' New York, but it was a fair way of saying thanks.

CARRIE (1952; b&w)

Director: William Wyler. *Writers:* Ruth and Augustus Goetz.

Unslakable love for a star-crossed, contradictory woman that leads to eventual ruin. The great Olivier, in one of his greatest film performances, using an American accent taught him by Spencer Tracy, is the increasingly unhinged lover; Jennifer Jones is his once-gained, then impossible object of desire. Another adaptation of a classic novel, Theodore Dreiser's *Sister Carrie,* this film was so strong and—we gather—so virulently downbeat in its original form that it was shelved for a year after its completion, then released in a truncated version that—according to Olivier—was also softened. What remains, however, is still extraordinary: Wyler's great contrast of spaciousness and claustrophobia, his formalism underscoring and holding in check—just barely—the fatalistic fervor of the story. Would this be what might happen, eventually, to Archer and Ellen if they broke convention, betrayed what they loved and believed of each other, and went away together? We talked over this possibility— and a few others—but dared draw no conclusions. The contours of Wharton's plot have their own rigorous resolution.

DETOUR (1945; b&w)

Director: Edgar G. Ulmer. *Writer:* Martin Goldsmith.

The kind of movie, resurrected and championed in the late '50s by the young film fiends of *Cahiers du Cinema,* that was used as a cudgel by skeptical American academics and hidebound reviewers to illustrate the folly of auteurism. *Detour,* along with most other Cahiers favorites, has endured, while the denunciations, if remembered at all, seem simply short-sighted and blind-sided. An image from *Detour* occurred to Marty while writing a scene of Archer receiving a note that would effect him deeply, and turn the plot sharply. Marty flashed on *Detour*'s existential schmo hero ruing his fate while the screen grew dark around him, until only his eyes were vivid in a single band of light. The light looked as if it had been filtered through the small rectangular window of a cell door in the solitary block. It was a bravura stylistic coup, but *Detour* has, on reflection, a bit more than a trick of the light in common with *Age.* Its grisly noir theatrics and all the conflated inventiveness of Ulmer's direction were at the service of a story, like *Age,* of two women and a man entangled in the unforgiving geometry of their own ardor. *Age,* on its surface, might have more elegance, but we'd count ourselves lucky to cut into some portion of *Detour*'s corrosive intensity.

EXPERIMENT PERILOUS (1944; b&w)

Director: Jacques Tourneur. *Writer:* Warren Duff.

A romantic thriller, set in the late Edwardian era in New York, with suggestions—like *Gaslight*—of dark doings in a marriage and dank obsessions lurking in the enfolding recesses of a great New York house. Tourneur was a master of unforced atmosphere: the menace here is almost palpable, but it never becomes too pronounced, even when the mystery is resolved in a way that's less imaginative than its meticulous creation. More shafts of light furnishing Marty with ideas: we hit the VCR to look over Tourneur's craftsmanship on several occasions, paying particular attention to the ways in which he used setting to reinforce atmosphere, not just to establish it. There was something almost—literally—dreamy in Tourneur's best movies, whether he was working in the realm of fantasy (*Cat People*), noir (*Out of the Past*) or horror (*Curse of the Demon*), but, if these played like dreams, they never seemed distanced, over-rarified by style. Their true mystery was in their simplicity.

FAR FROM THE MADDING CROWD (1967; color)

Director: John Schlesinger. *Writer:* Frederic Raphael.

Another classically inspired love story, from another classic (Thomas Hardy) source, made with grace and care, with attention not only to period but also to the imperatives of emotion that lead four brilliantly wrought and acted characters (Julie Christie, Alan Bates, Peter Finch, Terence Stamp) through a maze of intersecting destinies. Struggles against an enclosed society's expectations, battles against predestination that leave no victors on any side: the heart does not always finds its way. The movie seemed—and still does—both of its period and very much of our time, even though its themes of love, expectation, and obligation are thought to be old-fashioned. When they are managed as well as they are here, however, we were relieved to realize that "old-fashioned" may merely mean "overlooked," and ready for rediscovery.

THE HEIRESS (1949; b&w)

Director: William Wyler. *Writers:* Ruth and Augustus Goetz.

Henry James' *Washington Square*, evolved into a hard-grained story of romance and repression in 19th-century New York by the same team that would go on to *Carrie*. Precision balance of tension is maintained as a courtship is played out as a possible con game, and the influence of Europe compromises—perhaps corrupts—the paralyzed rectitude of American society. Wyler shoots drawing rooms, ballrooms and dining rooms as if they were antechambers of the soul, each filled with deep shadow and stalks of light, each holding some possible secret about a mystery that can never be solved. The implosive devastation of this movie's final scene—Olivia de Havilland ascending the steps of her house, lamp in hand, her face like a Mayan mask, leaving Montgomery Clift outside, pounding at the door, shut out forever—was a touchstone for our adaptation of *The Age of Innocence*. *The Heiress* is devastating and memorable in a far deeper way than Wyler's more warmly remembered *Wuthering Heights* because it is less sentimental. A woman is desolated, a man destroyed: all according to the murderous clockwork precision of societal order and social expectation.

THE INNOCENT (1977; color),
THE LEOPARD (1963; color) and SENSO (1954; color)

Director: Luchino Visconti. *Writers of* The Innocent:
Suso Cecchi D'Amico, Enrico Medioli, Luchino Visconti. *Writers of* The Leopard: Luchino Visconti, Suso Cecchi D'Amico, Pasquale Festa Campanile, Enrico Medioli,
Massimo Franciosa. *Writers of* Senso: Suso Cecchi D'Amico, Luchino Visconti, Giorgio Prosperi, Carlo Alianello,
Giorgio Bassani, Tennessee Williams, Paul Bowles.

Visconti's supreme trilogy of political change and romantic dissolution in the 19th century. Some movies are
inspiring; others are daunting. For us, these were both.
When I passed the Wharton novel to Marty, I suggested
that in milieu, it might remind him a little of these three
great films. *The Leopard,* especially, was a movie Marty
had seen often over the years, almost as if the film itself
were an act of sensual mesmerism. These Visconti films
are all social pageants, on a vast scale that we could never
hope to equal with *The Age of Innocence.* It would, indeed,
have been inappropriate to try, just as it would have been
an act of overweening hubris to set out to best, beat, even
duplicate them. But *The Leopard* exerted an unremitting
fascination. We knew that the ballrooms of aristocratic
Sicily were a good deal different than the ballrooms of old
New York, and if by some chance a Sicilian ballroom had
found its way to this innocent age, it would have looked
as seemly as a big top tent on a Newport lawn. Still, we
couldn't forget the lush last sequence of *The Leopard,* any
more than we'd want to extinguish a cherished recurring
dream. Visconti remained crucial to us, not for scale or as-
piration, but for spirit. He had found a way to work with
period material—"classical era" material—that had stylistic breadth and psychological panache. There was nothing
safe, small, or simply pretty about these films. They had
true contemporary pitch as well as an evocative epochal
sense, great detail of mise-en-scène to match an unwavering sense of emotional grandeur that no one has ever
approached again.

THE INNOCENTS (1961, b&w)

Director: Jack Clayton. *Writers:* William Archibald, Truman Capote, John Mortimer.

Henry James again, this time a wonderful adaptation of *The Turn of the Screw* in which lurking late Victorian repression is embodied—or, rather, disembodied—in the specters that haunt a governess at a remote stately home. Few movies can match this one for sheer draughty terror and clinging menace. Few catch what we took to be the undertone of the time so tellingly. We had no ghosts, of course; but what the apparitions of the dead represent in *The Innocents* seemed a good point on which to sight our compass for *Age.* They are shades that spring from a stifled psyche, the issue of thoughts unspoken, feelings unexpressed and dreams that die in shame with the daylight. They were, for us, an expression of much that was deeply, secretly felt but never spoken in *Age.* And the house in *The Innocents,* with its endless hallways all leading deeper into darkness, was a full character, just as it was in Robert Wise's similar and also superb *The Haunting.* We hoped, in the same way, that each room in *Age of Innocence* would be some refraction of the people living in it.

JULES AND JIM (1961; b&w)
and TWO ENGLISH GIRLS (1972; color)

Director: Francois Truffaut. *Writers:* Francois Truffaut, Jean Gruault.

Texts for style: the flutterpunch editing; the roving, restless camera, never still; the narration, which broke rules by recounting how characters felt, and even, on occasion, describing what they were doing while they did it; the reliance on letters and notes and diaries, and the way they were presented. These films were more than an inspiration. We thought of them personally, intimately, as a kind of legacy. There was more for us within them than just style, however. *Jules and Jim* was liberating. We both saw it at an age that was not simply impressionable. We were frantic for exaltation, looking for a reflection of the fire we felt for filmmaking up on the screen. We found it in *Jules and Jim.* The movie reveled in cinema: it conveyed a giddy, unfettered joy in the process of filmmaking, as well as in all its possibilities. Those possibilities seemed, with Truffaut's eye, to be exactly what we felt, wanted and needed them to be: limitless. It was only later, after uncounted viewings, that we began to work into the depths of these two movies: the elegiac eroticism, the tremendous psychological tension, the tidal pull toward destruction from which the characters can't escape. As a small way of acknowledging debt and returning thanks, the name of the author of the two novels on which these films were based got tucked into *The Age of Innocence.* Truffaut—whose own name became too celebrated for easy inclusion—remains in *Age,* we hope, as a continual shaping presence, a guiding grace.

LETTER FROM AN UNKNOWN WOMAN (1948; b&w) and LOLA MONTES (1955; color)

Director: Max Ophuls. *Writer of* Letter: Howard Koch. *Writers of* Lola Montes: Max Ophuls, Annette Wademant, Franz Geiger.

Ophuls was the cinema's foremost romantic. Perhaps its utmost. There were many others—Frank Borzage comes first to mind—but none cut sentiment with a saving shot of cynicism like Ophuls. These two movies, his best known, combine worldliness and fabulism with a kind of reflexive melancholy: the characters here are creatures of fate whose fates—in both cases—rush them past folly toward doom. And, of course, there are those camera moves. Dazzling tracking shots, splendiferous sweeps around the set: all the action seems orchestrated to a single heartbeat. What wonders would Ophuls have accomplished in these days of the Steadicam? His films, however bittersweet, were all fashioned with a stylistic ebullience that made even the most somber of them shine with the joy of craft and the confidence of a storyteller giddy with his own skill.

MADAME BOVARY (1949; b&w)

Director: Vincente Minnelli. *Writer:* Robert Ardrey.

Certainly, on the surface, this must have seemed a classic Hollywood mismatch: one of the greatest of all musical directors, adapting one of the most scrupulously unadorned of novels, a certifiable masterpiece of supple observation and social portraiture. But Minnelli knew himself better than most. Either that, or he discovered another dimension here, because his film—even with an odd framing device of Flaubert, in the dock, defending his novel against charges of obscenity—captures all the longing and desperation and wrongheaded, hopeless romanticism of Bovary, the willfulness that is winning and punishing at once. Minnelli's direction surprises with its uninsistent audacity. The film has a great set-piece: a dance that becomes rhythmic, then unrelenting, then vertiginous, till the ballroom windows have to be broken to give the women air. Minnelli fashions this into the perfect metaphor for Bovary's shut-in, stifled soul. The dance sequence is not aimlessly spectacular, but an extension of all the turmoil inside its main character. And Ellen Olenska must surely have read Flaubert.

THE MAGNIFICENT AMBERSONS (1942; b&w)

Director-Writer: Orson Welles.

A mutilated masterpiece—the *Greed* of the sound era—that, even in its tattered state, holds a high ground that few other movies can scale. Orson Welles' voice over a black screen—"The magnificence of the Ambersons began..."—echoes in the memory as (we're willing to argue about this) the most seductive spoken invitation to the past in all movie history. *Ambersons* has been a particular obsession since I first saw it, on WOR New York's Channel 9, on a program called "Million Dollar Movie." For any movie-smitten kid in New York, "Million Dollar Movie" was a living-room Cinematheque. It showed the RKO library once a night, twice on weekends—seven showings in all. Seven chances to see *King Kong* and *Bringing Up Baby* and *Gunga Din.* Seven chances, every one of them taken, to see *Citizen Kane.* And *Ambersons.* I was enthralled at the narrative sweep and stylistic virtuosity, the sheer voluptuous beauty of the film. I'd already read in the one book of film history on the shelves of my Bronx public library that the movie had been taken away from Welles, re-edited by the studio and severely compromised. I could tell *Kane* was a better movie, certainly more fully rounded and realized. I also knew, but could not work out why, I was more moved by *Ambersons* even than *Kane.* Marty shared much of my fascination, but not my full feeling. He admitted, at first, to being disappointed and confused by *Ambersons* after luxuriating in the finished pleasures of *Kane.* He was always troubled by the narrative and emotional gaps in *Ambersons,* its truncated rhythms and abrupt shifts of characterization. He could see its promise and potential, but the film—as well as its characters and milieu—remained a little alien to him. I recognized all these flaws in *Ambersons,* but loved the movie not only despite them, but, in another way, because of them: I could fill in the gaps myself, re-direct the movie in my own imagination toward the perfection I was certain that Welles, left free, would have achieved. I hectored Marty constantly about this, and, after a while, may have succeeded in getting him to see the movie a little bit my way. Our discovery of the Criterion laser-disc edition of *Ambersons,* which contained a script, stills, and descriptions of deleted scenes, as well as a second-channel audio narration that explained what was missing and where it went, both crimped our imagination and confirmed the feeling that *Ambersons,* after *Kane,* would have been the greatest one-two punch in movie history, a sure knockout. And, as it always had, *Ambersons* set us dreaming again.

MADELEINE (1949; b&w)

Director: David Lean. *Writers:* Nicholas Phipps, Stanley Haynes.

Maybe we're just being contrary. David Lean poormouthed this movie something awful, treating it as an unrelieved embarrassment. Certainly it's an anomaly in a career that seemed to treat each fresh venture as some new, splendid exploration, as if Lean were last in the line of great 19th-century adventurers, bushwhacking with crew and camera instead of rifle and porters. *Madeleine* was decidedly a side trip, not a safari, a side show in a life full of pageant. But, like a carny on the far side of a cathedral, it exerts its own peculiar, compulsive, and slightly naughty fascination. The movie is full of penumbra and nightshade, an appropriate combination for a high melodrama involving passion and poison in the last great days of the Empire. Lean's bleak, frosty fascination with murder as fit retribution as well as orgasmic release gives the film a nippy and welcomely disreputable undercurrent. Ann Todd's blank blonde stare lingers in close-up like a Victorian cameo hand-painted by Whistler and shaped by Tussaud.

THE PICTURE OF DORIAN GREY (1945; b&w) and THE PRIVATE AFFAIRS OF BEL AMI (1947; b&w)

Director-Writer: Albert Lewin.

Stuffed to bursting with literary importance and almost painfully self-conscious about their pedigree, Lewin's films are not as serious as they mean to be, but more fun than they seem. *Dorian Grey* is a perfervid mounting of the Wilde tale, propelled by an odd combination of textual reverence, winningly over-the-top acting, and static direction. Lewin always seemed leery of moving his camera, as if nothing should detract from the primary importance of the plummy dialogue. But his movies resonate with keen melodramatic vigor. *Bel Ami,* from de Maupassant, is, the opening title announces, "the history of a scoundrel." Played by George Sanders—who else? who better?—this lowlife snakes his way through the salons and bedrooms of 1880 Paris. "My heart tells me that you're right," he tells one of his protesting paramours. "But I haven't listened to my heart for a long time." He romances the widow of his best friend while the pillow still shows the outline of the deceased's head; he puts the make on the wife of a blind musician at the very door of Notre Dame while the husband pumps away at the organ inside; he becomes, in short, the rage and preeminent rake of society...sort of a Julius Beaufort, with more artifice and even less scruple. In one memorable moment, this rogue reads a fervid declaration of love from one of his female admirers while shaving. As we hear her voice-over rising in furious declarations of passion, he wipes his razor on her billet-doux. High style.

THE SPIRAL STAIRCASE (1946; b&w) and
THE STRANGE AFFAIR OF UNCLE HARRY (1945; b&w)

Director: Robert Siodmak. *Writer of* Spiral: Mel Dinelli. *Writers of* Uncle Harry: Stephen Longstreet, Keith Winter.

Two more heady plunges into the dank Victorian psyche; film noir in period, but totally in character. *Uncle Harry* features George Sanders again and poison again. It suggests, with a nice undertow of humor, that the only way to find true love in such an ordered, arranged, and muffled world is to murder for it. Hysteria is the keynote of *The Spiral Staircase.* The heroine is, literally, made mute by it, and by the ever-lurking presence of sexual violence. A conventional mystery in outline, Siodmak brings the story deeper into metaphor by using lots of German Expressionist chiaroscuro and some exquisite parlor tricks. At one point early on, he almost literally plunges into the killer's eye. Siodmak doesn't even bother with securing the polite veneer of middle-class Victorian America. This world, from the first, is a nightmare.

THE TOMB OF LIGEIA (1965; color)

Director: Roger Corman. *Writer:* Robert Towne.

Lurid and loopy: degenerate romanticism carried past all reasonable extremities. But reasonable movies are no good at all. *The Tomb of Ligeia* amounts to a minor but hardy compulsion, having first appeared in the *Mean Streets,* where it stoked the fantasies of the neighborhood guys. This canny adaptation has little to do directly with Poe. Our Wharton rendering, by comparison, is a model of fidelity, a near transcription. But as Corman and Towne capture the deranged meter of Poe's malarial imagination, we hoped—and tried—to find a space we could comfortably inhabit within Wharton's orderly architecture. Maybe writing *Age* was not really a matter of adaptation, then. It was more a process of personalization, and then re-discovery. And, always, of learning lessons, and trying not to forget.

Voices

It is not given to every one to be brilliant and amusing, but, with a little thought, passing events may always give rise to pleasant conversation. We have lately been visited by a succession of brilliant sunsets, concerning which there have been various theories. This has been a charming subject for conversation, yet at the average dinner we have heard but few persons mention this interesting topic.

—*Mrs. John F. Sherwood*, Manners and Social Usages, *1887*

Michael Ballhaus, M.S., Jay Cocks

M.S., Daniel Day-Lewis, Winona Ryder

There are not unfrequently substantial reasons underneath for customs that appear to be absurd.

—*Charlotte Bronte*

For my scenes we shot in a mansion in the Park Slope area of Brooklyn. The rooms of the house were not particularly large. As a consequence, Scorsese, with Jay Cocks and Michael Ballhaus at his side, watched the scenes on a monitor in an adjacent room. Scorsese was sensitive to the fact that he was physically removed from the actor, and thus, after a take, he would quickly appear and give his directions in a spirited, considerate and concise manner. He talked of things like pace and gesture. He remarked that for him doing *The Age of Innocence* was something of an anthropological study.

—*Norman Lloyd, Actor*

Most helpful in my research were the notes of Edith Wharton herself, remembering the speech and education of her parents' generation. Stressing that English, not American, was the language spoken by New York society in those days, she notes that children, both at home and in school, were educated by English nannies and teachers, the men usually spending a year or two at English universities.

—*Tim Monich, Dialogue Coach*

Only the sound of horses, fires, rustling dresses, and soft-spoken dialogue could fill the air. Blocking out the 1990s and re-creating the 1870s became a whole company affair. We had windows blocked with lead-lined foam, heating and phone systems shut down, contacts made with the airports to monitor flight paths, fireplaces designed to look real and operate as silently as possible, and a crew that moved on eggshells.

—*Tod Maitland, Production Mixer*

Behavior was different in those days: everyone, men and women alike, was taught to sit and stand without drawing attention to themselves; to be easy with their bodies, not fidgety; to understand stillness. If an actor can be taught that walking with a cane was a practical art, that a man used it as quiet punctuation as he walked, that the cane became a part of his body and added grace to it—this detail deepened the picture of the tenor of the times. If an actress could see that a fan was not necessarily used to show off but could be used to cool herself sparingly—it too would become part of what she was wearing rather than an out-of-place prop.

—*Lily Lodge, Etiquette Consultant*

Real politeness is the outward expression of the most generous impulses of the heart. If politeness is but a mask, as many philosophers tell us, it is a mask which will win love and admiration, and is better worn than cast aside.

—*Cecil B. Hartley,* The Gentleman's Book of Etiquette and Fashion, *1872*

When I first met Marty I gave him a letter with a few notes about the three aspects I thought were essential for the production design. There were 65 sets, but I felt, in them all, one or more of these elements was vital: color, which characterized the moods and personalities; painting, which portrayed the characters of the people who owned them; and food. There are seven dinner scenes in the film, and each of them is dramatically crucial.
—*Dante Ferretti, Production Designer*

This was all a new world for me: not only the world of Wharton, but working in America for the first time, too. But I believe that, whatever the place and whenever the time, a personal mode of dressing reflects a person's way of thinking, as well as character and social class. All the people who populated the story became, after a while, my companions, and soon, very soon, I started to feel at home in my new worlds.
—*Gabriella Pescucci, Costume Designer*

M.S., Dante Ferretti

Gabriella Pescucci, M.S

M.S, Michelle Pfeiffer

Mrs. Archer's Thanksgiving

Farewell dinner for the Countess

Cheerful conversation makes a successful meal. It always is a first aid to good digestion. Each member at the table is responsible for proper conversation.

—*M. E. W. Sherwood,*
The Art of Entertaining, *1893*

At The New-York Historical Society, I found so many books on etiquette and manners covering everything from 21 ways to eat strawberries to the correct angle for the fork to enter your mouth. I mainly worked on how to use the knife and fork properly and not to stick my elbows out.

—*Carolyn Farina, Actress*

I was supposed to put the dog I was holding down on the ground and take the parasol that Daniel was handing to me. But the dog decided to climb over my shoulder, down my back, and sit on my bustle. I tried to be polite and professional and do the right thing by going on with the scene, because no one called "Cut." But no one could keep a straight face except for Daniel, who teased me. "Why aren't you going on with the scene, why aren't you concentrating?"

—*Domenica Scorsese, Actress*

On my first day, Daniel and I did an after-dinner dialogue scene on a small library set. We had to smoke cigars...and *clip* them with beautiful Victorian clippers...and *light* them...and appear to *enjoy* them. Because Martin Scorsese is a perfectionist (an *affectionate* perfectionist), by the end of the day we had got through seventy cigars. Dammit, I was hooked!

—*Alec McCowen, Actor*

Coming on to the picture at the very end of the shooting was intimidating, but I was enveloped by a vibrant creative energy. I was immediately swept back into the past. Even my button shoes suddenly felt comfortable.

—*Robert Sean Leonard, Actor*

Each family in the film had a dinner, a kind of gathering of the tribe. I sifted through dozens of styles of china and silver to accurately represent each family. Every historian I spoke to had an opinion about what social standing a particular piece represented. The pieces were beyond opulent—extraordinary. Their abundance and importance signified a very specific time in American history.

—*Robin Standefer, Visual Research Consultant*

I have often sighed, in looking back at my childhood, to think how pitiful a provision was made for the life of the imagination behind those uniform brownstone façades, and then have concluded that since, for reasons which escape us, the creative mind thrives best on a reduced diet, I probably had the fare best suited to me.

—*Edith Wharton, "A Little Girl's New York,"*
Harper's Bazaar, *March 1938*

To read a book or a script of a story from another time usually means leaving time travel to the imagination. To location manage a "period" motion picture is to literally be able to find and visit another time. Like a complex puzzle, New York in 1880 was actually a combination of interior and exterior locations in Troy, Philadelphia, Brooklyn, the Bronx, Long Island, Westchester and Manhattan. We found the places Edith Wharton wrote about in fraternity houses, yacht clubs, gravel pits, men's clubs and lawyers' restored homes. We found Boston in a Brooklyn park and Florida on Long Island.
—*Patricia Anne Doherty, Assistant Production Manager*

There is a time when every being drifts back to the past...to the age of innocence.
—*John Ottesen, Special Effects*

M.S., mid-production

Outside the Mingott house: Troy, N.Y.

183

"When I was a girl," Mrs. Archer used to say, "we knew everybody between the Battery and Canal Street; and only the people one knew had carriages. It was perfectly easy to place anyone then; now one can't tell, and I prefer not to try."

—*Edith Wharton,* The Age of Innocence, *1920*

The Paris honeymoon: Winona Ryder and Daniel Day-Lewis with M.S.

The characters were aristocrats, so the carriages had to be brass and gold and beautiful with tufted seat cushions and beveled glass. That was tough to come by, because not too many people restore carriages to their authentic design and colors. I had to retuft all the seats, because they were vinyl or leather. They used velours and crushed velvets. I had to do that, not just get the carriage.

—*Jim Mazzola, Property Master*

In the aviary: The Botanical Garden, the Bronx, N.Y.

I think society is a business; it becomes
so in its practical working, and you find
in it, as I have said, only the imperfec-
tions of our common nature.

—*M. E. W. Sherwood,* An Epistle to Posterity, *1897*

My costume and make-up tests revealed that my
breasts are large and pillow-like but too far down my
body: they had to be jacked up under my chins, and so
Gabriella Pescucci, the costume designer (who spoke very
little English at the beginning of the film, and quite a lot
at the end), and Barbara Matera, the costume maker, con-
structed a series of stunning dresses—huge, padded, and
gorgeous—majestic creations based on original photographs and models, which gave me both avoirdupois and
dignity, an unusual combination.

—*Miriam Margolyes, Actress*

The Fifth Avenue exteriors, with three hundred extras,
were shot with giant wind machines working. Getting
through the day without having dozens of mutton-chops
and handle-bar moustaches flying through the air like bats
was a miracle.

—*Allen Weisinger, Make-up Artist*

Miriam Margolyes

Making 23rd Street, Manhattan, in Troy, N.Y.

185

It was a great deprivation when we were obliged to give up candles for illuminating. Nothing could be prettier than the effect of a room prepared for an evening party, decorated with flowers and lighted with wax candles. Candle-light is the only artificial light by which beauty shows all its beauty—it even makes the plain less plain.

—*Clarence Cook,* The House Beautiful, *1881*

The Beaufort Ball begins

Michael Ballhaus had to evoke period lighting. The sets had to be lit by candles, fire, gas. Nothing could be casual. You couldn't just turn on a bulb.
—*Dennis Gamiello, Key Grip*

Since sets ultimately become the territory of the shooting crew and are dismantled as soon as shooting is completed, I've learnt not to become too attached to anything we build. The final product, of course, is not what is sitting on some sound-stage but what is photographed and appears on the screen.
—*Speed Hopkins, Art Director*

Roses all the way, with faint wiff of sulphur.
—*Siân Phillips, Actress*

The social season with Faust

Oh, how do you do, Mrs. Brown?" said Mrs. Tomkins. "If only I had known you were going to call I should have tidied up the drawing-room."

—*Edith Wharton, in her first story,*
written in 1873, at age 12

COLUMBIA PICTURES Presents:

A Cappa/De Fina Production
A Martin Scorsese Picture

Daniel Day-Lewis   Michelle Pfeiffer   Winona Ryder

The Age of Innocence

Casting by Ellen Lewis

Associate Producer • Joseph Reidy

Co-Producer • Bruce S. Pustin

Title Sequence by Elaine & Saul Bass

Music by Elmer Bernstein

Costume Designer • Gabriella Pescucci

Editor • Thelma Schoonmaker

Production Designer • Dante Ferretti

Director of Photography • Michael Ballhaus, A.S.C.

Based upon the novel by Edith Wharton

Screenplay by Jay Cocks & Martin Scorsese

Produced by Barbara De Fina

Directed by Martin Scorsese

Technical credits not available upon publication.

PRINCIPAL CAST

NEWLAND ARCHER	Daniel Day-Lewis
ELLEN OLENSKA	Michelle Pfeiffer
MAY WELLAND	Winona Ryder
MRS. WELLAND	Geraldine Chaplin
HENRY VAN DER LUYDEN	Michael Gough
LARRY LEFFERTS	Richard E. Grant
REGINA BEAUFORT	Mary Beth Hurt
TED ARCHER	Robert Sean Leonard
MR. LETTERBLAIR	Norman Lloyd
MRS. MINGOTT	Miriam Margolyes
SILLERTON JACKSON	Alec McCowen
MRS. ARCHER	Siân Phillips
RIVIERE	Jonathan Pryce
LOUISE VAN DER LUYDEN	Alexis Smith
JULIUS BEAUFORT	Stuart Wilson

The editor wishes to give very special thanks to researchers Tamara Malkin-Stuart, Joanne Belonsky, and Anne Kerman, for their unwavering dedication, and to Margaret Bodde, Raffaele Donato, and the entire staff of Cappa Productions, and is also grateful to Barbara Bridgers at the Metropolitan Museum of Art; Holly Hotchner, Dale Neighbors, and Diana Arecco at The New-York Historical Society; Polly Sartori and Bronwyn Jonker at Christie's; Margot Horsey at Schumacher; David McFadden at the Cooper-Hewitt Museum; David Montgomery; and the expert book production and design team of Tania Garcia, Eileen Max, and Joe Gannon.

Particular thanks from M.S. and J.C. to: Columbia Pictures, especially to Mark Canton, Sid Ganis, Gareth Wigan, Michael Nathanson, and Mark Gill, for all their enthusiasm and assistance; the people of Newmarket Press, particularly Esther Margolis and Keith Hollaman, who were forebearing, encouraging, and indulgent; to Nora Ephron, who took time on her own set to do a four-star interview with Jim Mazzola; and to Paul Nelson, for his fine eye and lapidary touch with a red pencil.

REMEMBERING OUR COLLEAGUE SPEED HOPKINS.

Acknowledgments

We gratefully acknowledge permission to reprint copyrighted material from the following sources. Numbers refer to pages in this book where text excerpts or illustrations appear.

From *The Age of Innocence* by Edith Wharton. Renewal copyright © 1948. Reprinted by permission of Charles Scribner's Sons, a division of Macmillan Publishing Company: 1, 16-7, 19, 22-3, 47, 50, 52, 60-1, 79, 184

Courtesy of Albright-Knox Art Gallery. James Jacques Joseph Tissot, *The Reception*, (*L'Ambitieuse*), attributed 1883-1885. Oil on canvas. 56" x 40". Albright-Knox Art Gallery, Buffalo, New York, Gift of Mr. William M. Chase, 1909: 31

Courtesy of Archive Photos: *Barry Lyndon*, 169; *The Innocents*, 173; *The Private Affairs of Bel Ami*, 176

Courtesy of Arthur Sanderson: 1, 83, 179

Courtesy of The Bettman Archive: ix, 2

Courtesy of The Bridgeman Art Library: 24-5, 51

Courtesy of British Film Institute. *The Tomb of Ligeia*, 177

Courtesy of The Brooklyn Museum. Jacques Doucet, *Evening Dress*, c. 1902. Silk, velvet and net; appliqued floral motifs, silk ribbon trim. The Brooklyn Museum 65.239.7. Gift of Mrs. Robert G. Olmsted and Constable MacCracken: 29

Courtesy of Christie's: 63

Courtesy of The Detroit Institute of Arts, Founders Society. Purchased with funds from Mr. and Mrs. Richard A. Manoogian and Beatrice Rogers Bequest Fund: 6

From *Dining in America: 1850-1890*, © 1987, ed. Kathryn Grover. Reprinted by permission of University of Massachusetts Press: 42

From *Edith Wharton: A Biography* © 1975 by R. W. B. Lewis. Reprinted by permission of HarperCollins Publishers: 8-9, 187

Courtesy of Hungarian National Gallery: 59

Courtesy of Janus Films: *Jules and Jim*, 173; *Two English Girls*, 173

Courtesy of The Kobal Collection: *Detour*, 170; *Far from the Madding Crowd*, 171; *The Innocent*, 172; *Lola Montes*, 174; *The Magnificent Ambersons*, 175; *The Spiral Staircase*, 177; *The Strange Affair of Uncle Harry*, 177

Courtesy of The Metropolitan Museum of Art. Wolfe Fund, 1913. Catharine Lorillard Wolfe Collection: 7

Courtesy of The Metropolitan Museum of Art. Wolfe Fund, Catharine Lorillard Wolfe Collection, 1927: vi

Courtesy of Museum of Fine Arts, Boston. Bequest of Edith, Lady Playfair: 6

Courtesy of National Portrait Gallery, London: 41

Courtesy of The New-York Historical Society: i, 3, 9, 11, 13, 15, 36, 45, 52, 54, 55, 61, 66, 71, 73, 75

Courtesy of Photofest: *Carrie*, 169; *Experiment Perilous*, 170; *The Heiress*, 171; *The Leopard*, 172; *Senso*, 172; *Letter from an Unknown Woman*, 174; *Madeleine*, 176; *The Picture of Dorian Gray*, 176

From a private collection: 19

From a private collection. Photograph courtesy Hazlitt, Gooden & Fox, London: 49

Courtesy of Schumacher: iii, 167

From the collection of Joey and Toby Tanenbaum, Toronto, Canada: 30

Courtesy of The Terra Museum of American Art: 57

Courtesy of Turner Entertainment: *Madame Bovary*, 174

From *Young in New York: A Memoir of Victorian Girlhood* © 1963 by Nathalie Dana. Reprinted by permission of Doubleday, a division of Bantam Doubleday Dell Publishing Group, Inc.: 66